KOS
NISYROS

ΕΚΔΟΣΕΙΣ
ΤΕΧΝΗ
EDITIONS

The Early Christian church of Ayios Stefanos at Kefalos and, opposite, the islet with the Monastery of Ayios Antonios.

Pages 4, 5
The coastal road along Cape Miaouli, with the characteristic Local Government Building.

Text: Giorgos Koukas, Miltiades Logothetes
Editor: Daphne Christou
Artistic Editor: Evi Damiri
Translation: Despina Christodoulou
Photographs: Michael Toubis S.A. Archives, Ioannis Tzartos
Colour separation, printing: M. TOUBIS GRAPHIC ARTS S.A.

Nisiza Karela, Koropi, Tel.: 010-6029974, FAX: 010-6646856
http://www.toubis.gr
ISBN: 960-540-438-9

We would like to thank Manolis Kiapokas (philologist), Georgos Sfikas (research on the natural environment) and Vasilis Tselepides (geology) for their contribution to the writing of this book..

Cafe-Snack
ΚΑΜΕΛΙΑ
Cocktail Bar

CONTENTS

1. KOS

2. HISTORICAL INTRODUCTION

3. CULTURE AND TRADITION

4. KOS TOWN

CONTENTS

5. ITINERARIES ON THE ISLAND

6. NISYROS

KOS

There are so many things that make us want to go to Kos, that to mention them alone would seem excessive. Kos is the island of healing, the island which pulled humanity out from the vanity created by ignorance and lack of learning. It is the island of Hippocrates, the father of medicine who gave medicine to man and the first hospitals, the first doctors, to the island.

The ruins and archaeological finds which have been excavated at various points of the island bring to life memories of a continuous civilisation of over six thousand years.

The traces of ancient prehistoric settlements, the ruins of the buildings of classical antiquity, the Hellenistic period and the Roman years, impressive Byzantine and post-Byzantine churches, imposing medieval castles, mosques and minarets alternate with the more recent contemporary buildings.

The beach at Mastihari, and the coastal road for the town.

On Kos, the need for change has meant that these traditional features have been absorbed in a creative fashion, whilst the natural environment justifies the most admiring eulogies.

The Kos of today is now one of the most modern summer resorts, without having lost all those things which, for other reasons, some centuries ago made the island stand apart. The hospitality, the smile and the willing service of the Koans are truly remarkable.

On Kos you can live as you choose. You can lose yourself in a noisy and carefree crowd or hide away on one of the island's deserted beaches. You can enjoy the sea and the mountain, or a pleasurable meal in a cosmopolitan restaurant and a coffee, in the company of the locals at one of their regular hang-outs.

You will be dazzled by the colours dancing in all possible combinations. Become entranced by the vibrant blue of the sky and the sea and then relax looking at the green which covers the island.

This is Kos. Beautiful, diverse, enchanting. And we are its captives.

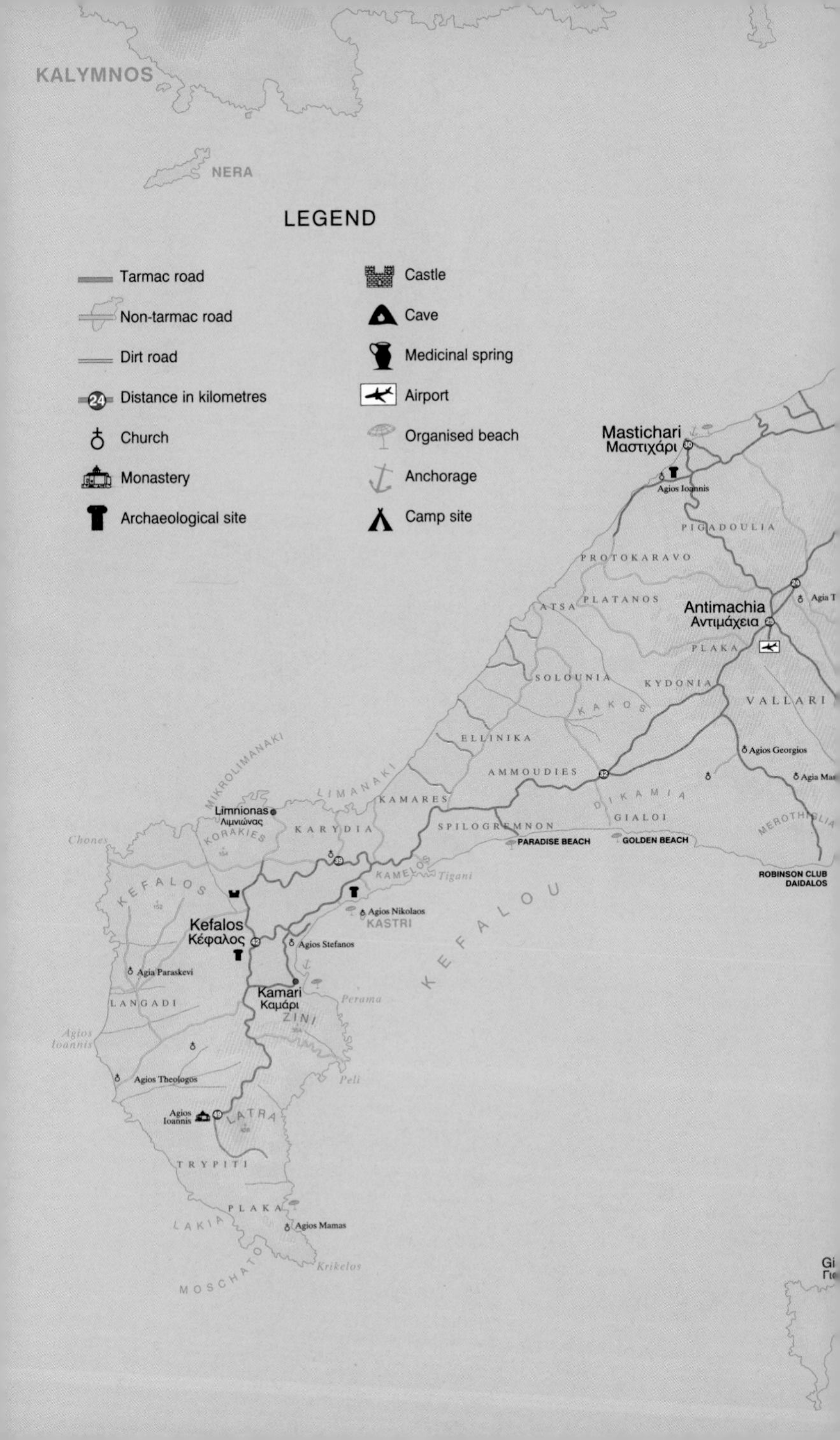

KALYMNOS
NERA
LEGEND
Tarmac road
Non-tarmac road
Dirt road
24 Distance in kilometres
Church
Monastery
Archaeological site
Castle
Cave
Medicinal spring
Airport
Organised beach
Anchorage
Camp site
Mastichari
Μαστιχάρι
Agios Ioannis
PIGADOULIA
PROTOKARAVO
PLATANOS
ATSA
Antimachia
Αντιμάχεια
PLAKA
SOLOUNIA
KYDONIA
KAKOS
VALLARI
ELLINIKA
Agios Georgios
AMMOUDIES
MIKROLIMANAKI
LIMANAKI
KAMARES
DIKAMIA
GIALOI
Limnionas
Λιμνιώνας
KARYDIA
SPILOGREMNON
PARADISE BEACH
GOLDEN BEACH
MEROTHIGLIA
ROBINSON CLUB DAIDALOS
Chones
KORAKIES
KEFALOS
KAMELOS
Tigani
KEFALOU
Agios Nikolaos
KASTRI
Kefalos
Κέφαλος
Agios Stefanos
Agia Paraskevi
Kamari
Καμάρι
Perama
LANGADI
ZINI
Agios Ioannis
Agios Theologos
Peli
LATRA
TRYPITI
PLAKA
LAKIA
Agios Mamas
MOSCHATO
Krikelos

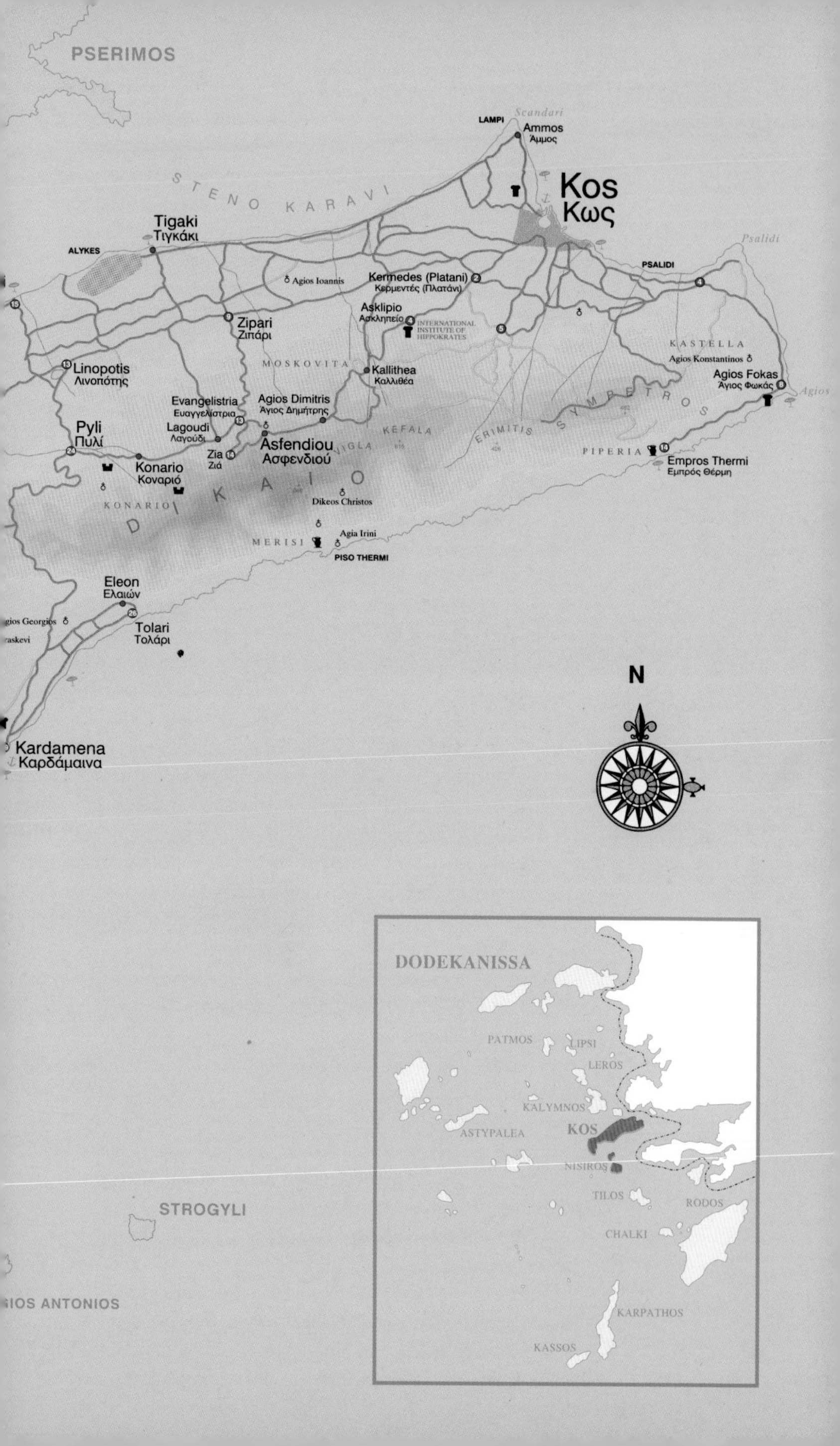

PSERIMOS
Scandari
LAMPI
Ammos
Άμμος
STENO KARAVI
Kos
Κως
Psalidi
Tigaki
Τιγκάκι
ALYKES
PSALIDI
Agios Ioannis
Kermedes (Platani)
Κερμεντές (Πλατάνι)
Asklipio
Ασκληπιείο
INTERNATIONAL INSTITUTE OF HIPPOKRATES
Zipari
Ζιπάρι
KASTELLA
Agios Konstantinos
Linopotis
Λινοπότης
MOSKOVITA
Kallithea
Καλλιθέα
Agios Fokas
Άγιος Φωκάς
Agios
Evangelistria
Ευαγγελίστρια
Agios Dimitris
Άγιος Δημήτρης
SYMPETROS
Pyli
Πυλί
Lagoudi
Λαγούδι
KEFALA
ERIMITIS
Zia
Ζιά
Asfendiou
Ασφενδιού
VIGLA
PIPERIA
Empros Thermi
Εμπρός Θέρμη
Konario
Κοναριό
DIKAIO
KONARIO
Dikeos Christos
Agia Irini
MERISI
PISO THERMI
Eleon
Ελαιών
Agios Georgios
Paraskevi
Tolari
Τολάρι
N
Kardamena
Καρδάμαινα
DODEKANISSA
PATMOS
LIPSI
LEROS
KALYMNOS
ASTYPALEA
KOS
NISIROS
TILOS
RODOS
CHALKI
KARPATHOS
KASSOS
STROGYLI
AGIOS ANTONIOS

Nature and Location

The Dodecanese are an emerald chain of islands in the Greek archipelago. Although their name means 'twelve islands', there are in fact many more: about 20 are inhabited, and the uninhabited islets are almost literally countless. The South Sporades, as the Dodecanese used to be called, are the continuation of the Cyclades, and they can boast an uninterrupted history of Greek civilisation. One of those emerald isles is Kos. Kos is one of the choicest islands in the Dodecanese, a real diamond, a blessed place. With an area of 290 square kilometres and a population of about 29.500, it is the third-largest island in the group, after Rhodes and Karpathos.

Kos lies to the south of Kalymnos and the north of Nisyros, off the mouth of the Gulf of Kos (the Kerameikos Gulf in ancient times, and known as Kerme Korferi in Turkish). It is some four miles off the coast of Asia Minor, has the general shape of a sickle with a very long handle, measures 45 kilometres in length and has a width varying from 2 to 11 kilometres. The section of the island which protrudes into the Gulf lies between the promontory of Halicarnassus (Bodrum) and that of Cnidus.

At some time, Kos must have been part of the large expanse of land which occupied what is now the Aegean Sea. The ancient Greeks, who knew of this continent, called it Aegeis. But geological upheavals rent Aegeis, sending some sections of it to the bottom of the sea and creating the Aegean archipelago - one part of which is the Dodecanese.

Morphology

From the point of view of its terrain, Kos can be divided into three zones: a) a chain of hills which begins at the south-east cape of Ayios Fokas and crosses to the south coast, where it ends at Kardamaina; b) a flat area in the north-west, as far as the sea, and c) another mountainous area in the south-west, along the Kefalos promontory. Kos has coasts of a total length of 112 kilometres, on which the most important bays are those of Kos, in the north-east, and the two bays to the north and south of Kefalos.

The names of the most important capes and headlands on Kos are Skandario (Koubourno), Psalidi, Ayios Fokas, Krikellos (Lakitiras), Gourniatis (Chelona) and Drepano.

The coastline plunges steeply into the sea in some places, while elsewhere it descends more gently to pretty bays and sandy beaches. Over the eastern section of the island and along its south coast towers the highest mountain, called Oromedon or Dikaios, whose topmost peak reaches 846 metres. The terrain is deeply riven with gorges and valleys, may of them very fertile and with numerous streams.

Kos has medicinal springs, such as the 'Embros Thermi' at Ayios Fokas, the Ayios Soulas spring, and the 'Piso Thermi' spring at Ayia Eirini. The island's salt-pan was one of the best in the Mediterranean, and the only one in the Dodecanese. Today, however, it is a preserved wetland. In the past there were mines on Kos (extracting copper, iron, lead, sulphur, lignite and galena). The mountainous regions are clothed in attractive woods.

The morphology of the terrain and the abundant supplies of water favour the production of high-quality agricultural produce, in considerable quantities. Kos grows cereals, fruit and vegetables. Stock-breeding, too, is highly developed, and much honey is made.

Administrative Division

Following the last law implemented for the administrative division of the island (the Capodistrias plan), Kos is divided into three Municipalities: 1) the Municipality of Kos includes the island's capital and its suburbs and has a population of 14,700, 2) the Municipality of Dikaios was created from the unification of the communities of Asfenidou and Pyli and has a population of 6,000, 3) the Municipality of Herakleios was created from the unification of the communities of Antimacheia, Kardamaina and Kefalos and has a population of 6,400..

Climate

Kos has a mild climate. From ancient times it has been characterised as 'a place pre-eminently temperate (Galen). The temperature very rarely rises above 35 degrees celsius in the summer months and rarely falls below 0 degrees in the winter. The north-east section of the island has plenty of waters and rich vegetation with little humidity, whilst the climate of the south-west section is dry. Callimachus characterised it as 'rich,' i.e. fertile, Strabo as 'fruitful' and Herondas as 'sweet,' whilst for Antonio Galateo it was a 'corculum mundi,' i.e. the little heart of the world. The annual sunlight exceeds 300 days.

Geology

Greece's oldest rocks can be seen on the island of Kos. Despite their age, these rocks have experienced only slight metamorphosis, and in which fossils dating to the Lower Palaeozoic period (approximately 345 million years ago) have been located. The lowest stratum of Kos, then, is composed of phyllites, pelites and micritic limestone with interjections of volcanic materials and marble. These rocks are over 2000 metres thick.

There follow newer rocks of the Mesozoic period which do not differ greatly from the rocks preceding, although these too contain fossils, on the basis of which we date them to the Mesozoic period. Overall, we can say that Kos is constituted of rocks the formation of which took over 350 million years.

After a dry period, most likely at the end of the Middle Mesozoic period (approximately 180 million years ago), new sediments followed, which again required a long period of time in which to form, perhaps even over 150 million years.

A characteristic feature of the island of Kos is that lava has drained into almost all the layers of rock. This volcanic lava appears to be of a different age, something which indicates that on different occasions there were volcanic eruptions in the region. The youngest volcano dates to the Pleistocene era, approximately over 200,000 years ago. Another characteristic of the island of Kos is that almost the whole of its west section is covered by later volcanic rock, the so-called rhyolites, which prevent the spread of older rock sediment, mainly Cretaceous limestone (75 million years old), as well as newer formations as late as the Pleistocene period (200,000 years ago).

In the central and eastern sections of the island there is a preponderance of older rocks in the south whilst there are more recent sediments in the north. It appears, then, that the northern section of the island remained under the sea for a much longer period whilst the south rose prematurely and, as a result, is not composed of newer rock. This premature rising may also have caused any new rock to have eroded, thus revealing the older rock beneath.

Kos did not escape the tectonic activity of Alpine orogenesis. Large sections of the island are thus covered by two different tectonic covers, one of which shows many possible features of the Gavrovos zone whilst the other, more recent, belongs to the so-called cover of the upper tectonic unit of Greece. There is, in other words, rock which was not formed in the region of Kos but which was transferred here by tectonic activity from other regions, and were pushed over the local rock of Kos.

The Natural Environment

In the prehistoric era Kos must have been covered with thick forest which began to recede once man settled on the island, at the beginning of the Neolithic period. Today the vegetation is significantly reduced with dry bushes prevailing over a large part of the island. Shrubs and crops can be seen in some places.

Today the only significant forest area to be found is on Mt Dikios, with pine (Pinus brutia) and cypress (Cupressis sempervirens) trees. Some of these trees have grown naturally whilst the rest are the result of reforestation. These forests would certainly be more extensive if there was no grazing of sheep and goats, which stymies their natural regrowth.

Flamingos can often be seen at Tingaki.

As is only natural, the fauna, flora and nature of Kos have not remained uninfluenced by the neighbouring region of Asia Minor. The flora incudes almost 1000 different species of plant, many of which are common all over the Eastern Mediterranean, such as the various species of rockrose (Cistus), the various species of poppy (Papaver), the two species of anemone (Anemone coronaria and Anemone pavonina), the wild gladioli (Gladiolus italicus), the chrysanthemums (Chrysanthemum coronarium) the sea daffodil (Pancratium maritimum), the wild violets (Malcolmia flexuosa, Matthiola sinuata and Matthiola tricuspidata) and the wood sorrel (Oxalis pes-caprae).

Aside from those common to the whole region, there are some rare species of plant with an Asian origin, such as the Phlomis lycia, the Dianthus elegans, the Silene urvilei, the Jurinea consanguinea, etc.

Other notable plants are the Campanula lyrata, the Alkanna orientalis, the Caslystegia soldanella, the Achillea cretica, the

Mandragora autumnalis and the Asterolinon linum-stellatum. We should also mention that at least 22 different species of orchids have so far been found on the island.

As for the fauna, we should first mention that Kos is located on the path taken by migrating birds. In the spring and autumn, then, one can see many rare species, such as the oriole (Oriolus oriolus), the European bee-eater (Merops apiaster), the European roller (Coracias garrulus), the hoopoe (Upupa epops) and various species of heron (Ardea). On Mt Dikios birds of prey can also be seen, such as the Bonelli's Eagle (Hieratus fasciatus) and the long-legged buzzard (Buteo rufinus), whilst the extremely rare Asian species of the Blue-cheeked bee-eater (Merops superciliosus), one of the most beautiful birds of Western Asia, sometimes makes an appearance.

Every spring swallows and swifts come to the island from Africa and nest. The barn swallow (Hirundo rustica), with the long, scissors-like tail, and the house martin (Delichon urbica), with the brilliant-white stomach, build their nests out of mud beneath the roofs and balconies, whilst the swifts (Apus) prefer to hide away in the chimneys of old houses.

There are two small yet interesting wetlands in Kos: the salt-pan at Tingaki, on the north coast, and the marsh in the region of Psalida, on the east coast. Rare birds can on occasion be seen at both these wetlands, such as the Greater Flamingo (Pheonicopterus ruber) and the glossy ibis (Plegadis falcinellus), whilst the tortoises Caretta caretta and Chelonia mydas come out to lay their eggs along the sandy beach at Tingaki.

In the winter many wetland birds from northern and eastern Europe come to these regions to pass the winter, during which time the visitor will be able to see various species of duck and even swans.

The region which encompasses the salt-pan of Tingaki, Mt Dikios and the Psalidi marsh has been designated protected and is part of NATURA 2000, the European Union's network of protected natural environments.

The lake at Linopoti.

HISTORICAL INTRODUCTION

The columns of the Temple of Apollo in the Asklepeion.

The name of Kos

Kos has jealously guarded its name, and has kept it the same since the earliest times. The other names it was given - such as Meropis or Karis - were soon forgotten. But everything stands witness to the history of the island, which is lost in the mists of time.
Some scholars believe that the name Kos comes from that of a princess, daughter of King Triops II or King Meropas II: she was called Koos, and thus Kos by elision. Another possibility is the derivation from the Karian word 'koion', meaning sheep, either because the shape of the island resembled a sheep or because there were numerous sheep on it. A third school traces the name to the word 'kos', meaning an enclosure or a crab (and indeed crabs are often depicted on the ancient coins of the island).

However, we know that it also had other old names: Meropis, Meropeis and Merope, from the mythical king Meropas. Among other ancient names were Karis (from its proximity to the Karian race) and Nymphaea (from its reputedly large population of nymphs).

In the Middle Ages, the Knights of St John called Kos Lango for a while, and in 1389 we find it under the name Nerantzia, thanks to its abundance of citrus trees. In Turkish times, it was known as Stanko, from a corruption of the phrase 'stin Ko', i.e. 'in Kos'.

Among the names mentioned by other scholars are Kynnis (from the Titan Cynnus), Karis (not from the Karians this time, but from an ancient word for shrimp - because of the shape of the island), the Isle of the Blessed (because of its prosperity) and Makrya ('long', from its shape, and here there may be a connection with the medieval Lango).

The plane-tree of Hippocrates in the central square of Kos, engraving by J.B. Hiliare (Gennadios Library).

Mythology

Kos seems to have been inhabited in Neolithic times: finds from this period have come to light in the Aspropetra cave near Kefalos. This means that the first inhabitants settled there in the mid-4th millennium BC.

Many of the myths of the ancient Greeks refer to the settlement of Kos and to events which took place there in prehistoric times. According to once such tradition, the Giants who were the offspring of Uranus and Gaia fled when they were defeated in their terrible battle against the gods of Olympus. The god Poseidon set off in pursuit of the Giant Polybotes: as they passed Kos, he snipped off a piece of the island with his trident and threw it at his quarry, killing him. The severed piece formed the neighbouring islet of Nisyros. Here, quite clearly, we can see the myth being used as a way of explaining the natural truth that Nisyros had once been a part of Kos.

Another myth involving the Giants tells us that the Giants Coeos, Phoebus and Cynnus took refuge on Kos and some scholars derive the ancient names Kos and Kynnis from the first and third of these figures.

There are other myths, too, about Kos and its inhabitants. They tell of the many heroes and demigods who visited the island (including Achilles with his father Peleus). Behind these visitors we can discern the movements of populations, who came to Kos in a succession of waves as conquerors or peaceful settlers. The first true settlers of the island must have been Pelasgians and Leleges. Perhaps they found a more primitive native population there, to whom they taught their accomplishments in the crafts and in farming. Among their creations were the megalithic Cyclopean Walls of which traces have survived down to the present. Later, some time in the second millennium BC, Karians arrived on the island from nearby, Asia Minor.

The colonists of this period were called Triopes and Meropes in the myths, and there is a tradition that the name of their first king was Meropas.

As is usually the case, the mythological tradition is confused and confusing. According to one version, King Triopas, who was descended from the Meropes and Triopes together, became leader of the Karians and brought them to the east coast of Kos. There, in the vicinity of modern Ayios Fokas, they built the city of Triopos.

Triopas was succeeded by his son Meropas, who extended Karian sovereignty to the entire island, which took his name and was now called Meropis (and its inhabitants Meropes).

Another myth tells us that the gallant and creative Meropes built the island's first city in very ancient times and gave it the name of King Meropas' daughter, Astypalaea.

Of course, we do not really know which city was founded first, or who was its king. The myths contain the names of many leaders of the Meropes, such as Meropas himself, Phaethon, Koos, Meropas son of Hyan, Meropas son of Coos Prophthan, Meropas king of Kos Eumelus, Meropas Hyperphan, Meropas son of Triopas king of Kos, and so on.

If we follow a different path through the mythological tangle, we shall end up in quite another place.

The successor to Meropas the first, according to this version, was Triopas the second.

He was succeeded by Meropas the second, whose daughter was called Koos (and Kos by elision). Some scholars connect the name of the island with this princess.

In the great years of Minoan Crete, King Minos II, although he ruled almost all the Mediterranean and had driven the Karians out of most of the islands, chose to leave the islanders of Kos alone and to maintain a long friendship with them.

Triopas the third was succeeded by his son Eudaemon. The next king was Eurypylos, husband of the beautiful Clytia and father of Chalcon, who in turn became king and built the famous fountain of Vourina.

After the Flood (of Deucalion, in the Greek myths) - that is, around 1500 BC - Kekrops set out from the Egyptian colony of Sais and called at

Kos on his way to Attica, leaving a batch of colonists on the island. Shortly afterwards, Danaos, whose journey - with his fifty daughters - had begun in Upper Egypt, settled at Argos and became the founding father of the house of Perseus. The myths tell us that Kos was associated with this house.

Later, around 1300 BC, Thepolemus, son of Heracles and Astychoe, king of Rhodes (which was an Argive and Athenian colony), extended his power to Kos.

Clash between a young gladiator and a tiger. Late Hellenistic mosaic floor. Archaeological Museum of Rhodes.

The story of the colonisation of Kos by the family of Herakles (the Heraklids) is extremely confused but highly interesting. It has to be disentangled from the web of myths surrounding the hero and demigod Herakles.

According, then, to this myth, after Herakles had performed his twelve famous feats he was ordered to do some more by the cousin of King Eurystheus. They were all easier and less important, but one of them was to free Hesione, daughter of King Laomedon of the Troad, from the rock to which she was pinioned as prey to a sea monster. Herakles slew the monster, but Laomedon cheated him out of his reward. In wrath, Herakles laid waste to the Troad and set sail for home in six ships laden with booty.

Five of these vessels sank in a fearful storm. Herakles and some of his comrades managed to survive, and were washed up as castaways on the cape of Kos now known as Gourniatis. As they walked into the hinterland, they met a shepherd called Antagoras, who was grazing his sheep. Herakles asked Antagoras to let them have one of his sheep, for which he was prepared to pay. But Antagoras - who was renowned for his strength - replied roughly, challenging the stranger to fight: if he won, the sheep would be for nothing.

Although Herakles was exhausted after the hardships of his voyage and half-dead with hunger, he accepted the challenge. The wrestling bout lasted many hours, and first Herakles, then Antagoras, seemed to be on the point of victory.

In the meantime, news of the fight had spread, and many islanders flocked to watch. Seeing Herakles gaining the upper hand, they tried to help Antagoras.

This enraged Herakles' comrades, and a general free-for-all developed. Feeling his fatigue overcoming him, Herakles withdrew from the combat, while his comrades scattered into the surrounding hills. The demigod took refuge in a house belonging to a woman from Thrace, and he had to disguise himself as a woman.

The story reached the ears of King Eurypylus, who took Herakles for a pirate and ordered his arrest. Still in women's clothes, Herakles fled by night to a mountain fortress near Pyli, which since then has been called Phyxa or Pyxa (from 'phyge', meaning flight).

Before long, the hospitable inhabitants of the surrounding area discovered who was living in their midst, and they recognised that he was right to accuse Eurypylus and his servants of breaking the laws governing the treatment of strangers. They joined Herakles in his campaign against the king. In the battle between the two sides, Chalcon, son of Eurypylos, wounded Herakles, but the demigod slew his father and took captive Chalcon's sister Chalcione. Herakles married Chalcione and recognised Chalcon as his lawful successor, before sailing on to Folegandros. The marriage of Herakles and Chalcione produced Thessalos, who became king of Nisyros and the northern islands called the Kalydnes (Leros and Kalymnos). Thessalos' sons Antiphos and Pheidippos were the leaders of the detachment of thirty ships which the islands of Kos, Kalydnes, Nisyros, Karpathos and Kasos sent to join the Achaean campaign against Troy.

All these mythological references to Herakles and his adventures are bound up with the movements of Greek peoples (Karians and Dorians) through the island. The link with the Heraklids was an attempt to explain the close bonds which developed between Kos and the people of Thessaly as far back as the second millennium BC.

We are reminded of the Karians and the Pelasgians by the ruins of the Cyclopean walls at the Vourina fountain, Palaioskala and Ayios Fokas, and in the place names Halasarna and Astypalaia.

Mosaic floor showing Poseidon overpowering the giant Polybotes. Archaeological Museum of Rhodes.

Prehistoric Period (4000 - 800 π.Χ.)

We have already noted that the first Neolithic settlement on Kos dates back to the fourth millennium BC. The inhabitants of the island during the Bronze Age (that is, from about 3000 BC to approximately 1500 BC) lived in and around caves, tilling the soil.

Apart from the Greek tribes, the Phoenicians also came to Kos. Some tombs which have been found on the eastern side of the island are evidence that the Phoenicians passed on to the islanders the custom of burying jewellery with their women.

In around 1600 BC a Minoan colony from Crete was established in the part of the modern town of Kos now known as Serayia. This was only natural, as the sea-faring Minoans would need Kos harbour for trade with the coast of Asia Minor. However, relations between the settlers and the locals seem to have remained on a friendly basis, and Kos did not become politically or socially dependent on the Minoans.

When the important centres of the Minoan civilisation were destroyed and Crete was laid waste, the Myceneans took over all their colonies and set up an empire of their own, with their version of civilisation.

Traces of nine Mycenean cities have come to light in Kos. The most important of these was the one which stood on the site of the earlier Minoan settlement, now called Serayia. It was dependent on Rhodes, but traded extensively with parts of Asia Minor (Anatolia), Syria and Egypt.

The role played by Kos and the neighbouring islands, with their 30 ships, in the Trojan War is related by Homer in the Iliad. Homer also tells us that after the fall of Troy Pheidippos and Antiphos, the Heraklid commanders of the fleet, sank on their voyage home. Pheidippos and his companions survived and were washed up on Andros, while Antiphos was swept across the Aegean to a Pelasgic land called Thessaly, of which he became king.

Among the castaways who were washed up on Kos after the fall of Troy was Podaleirios, son of Asklepios, with his band of companions. This, according to the myth, was the beginning of the cult of Asklepios the Healer on Kos. However, there is another myth which attributes the establishment of the cult to later settlers from Epidaurus in the Peloponnese.

When the Mycenean empire went into decay, the Dorians spread throughout the Greek lands and had soon penetrated to even the most isolated corners once ruled by the Achaeans. In time, they came to Kos, where the Doric dialect and Doric script came to predominate.

Under the Dorians the island flourished in agriculture, handicrafts, shipping and trade. Strabo tells us that Kos and Rhodes founded colonies together: Elpies in Lower Italy was an example.

Ancient Religious Cults

The cults of Asklepios the Healer and of Herakles were particularly popular in Kos. To honour the founder of medicine, the islanders held magnificent ceremonies and offered rich sacrifices.

The rites in honour of Herakles were no less splendid. It was customary at these ceremonies for the chief priest to wear the estheta, a woman's garment, with a richly decorated mitre on his head. This was in commemoration of Herakles' mythical escape in women's dress from the men of Eurypylus who were pursuing him.

Of course, other gods were also worshipped on Kos among them being Apollo, Zeus, Dionysius, Demeter (for whom there was a major festival, the Thalysia), Aphrodite and Hera.

The Ancient Demes

The first capital of Kos was the city of Astypalaia. According to scholars, it stood on the spot now known as Palatia, on the coast near the village of Kefalos.

In the earliest times the island was ruled by kings. Later, however, hereditary monarchy was abandoned in favour of a system of rule by archons, initially appointed for life, then for a period of ten-years and latterly for a year.

In the 7th and 6th centuries, the political institutions of the entire Greek world entered a period of radical change. The people of Kos embraced progressive ideas and eventually compelled their archons to transfer their power to the 'ekklesia of the demos', or assembly of the people. This introduced democracy to the island, and a senate and parliament were formed. The head of state was called a monarch, and his role was largely honorary and priestly. Executive power was in the hands of the six 'prytaneis' or chief magistrates, assisted by their secretary, the general (or generals), the admiral, the officers and the captains of triremes. Public accountants, policemen, guards of public property, debt collectors, market policemen and judges were appointed. The schools were staffed with teachers paid by the parents of the pupils, while the deme looked after the fees of poorer children. The Koans were particularly proud of the winners of public athletic contests, held in separate categories for boys, adolescents and men. These events and the celebrations to mark them were controlled by the gymnasiarch, and there was a trainer to look after the practice sessions. The kithara players, an instrument similar to a harp, were responsible for public musical events, and there were state officials to supervise education.

The statue of the goddess Hygeia with the snake and Eros at her feet, 2nd century BC. Archaeological Museum of Kos.

Persian Rule

Towards the end of the 6th century BC the Persians extended their empire and incorporated the Greek cities of Asia Minor into it as satrapies. From there, of course, the next step was to the islands lying just off the coast, and so Kos became a satrapy too. To begin with, relations with the Persians were perfectly friendly, despite the fact that they came as conquerors and had economic demands to make. But when it became clear that the Persians were preparing to launch an attack on mainland Greece and that their 'allies' would have to take part in it, Kos refused to help the vast Persian fleet. The Persians became angry, occupied the island and gave it to Artemisia the Elder, queen of Halicarnassus. She was a loyal ally of the Persians, and had been recognised as queen of Karia. As a result, five ships were built on Kos on Artemisia's orders and joined the Persian fleet.

After the defeats at Salamis and Plataeae, and once the remainder of the Persian fleet had been annihilated at Mycale, Kos and the other Greek cities and islands were free of the Persian yoke for ever.

Athens or Sparta?

In 477 Kos became allied with Delos, and later it joined the Athenian League. The size of the island's annual contribution to the League's common treasury gives some idea of the prosperity and power of Kos at this time. Although the bonds between Kos and the Dorians dated a very long way back, the islanders found themselves on the Athenian side when the Peloponnesian War broke out in 431. Of course, there was some resistance to this among the oligarchic party on the island, and there were short periods when Kos made approaches to the Spartan side.

In the winter of 413-412 BC, a fearful earthquake flattened much of Kos. In 411 a Spartan fleet under admiral Astyochos appeared off Astypalaia, the capital. Although the islanders made gestures of welcome, the Spartans occupied the city, looted it and took much booty away with them. Many islanders were forced to flee and settle on another island nearby to the south-west, which they renamed Astypalaea. Others moved to the far end of the island, where there were already settlements near the Asklepeion and at Cape Skandario. Their numbers were such that, under the instructions of the priests of Asklepios, they built a whole new city: Kos, the capital of the island. When the Athenians heard of the havoc which the earthquake had wrought, followed by the disaster of the Spartan raid, they sent out their admiral, Alkibiades, with a flotilla of ships carrying supplies and money. Alkibiades helped the Koans build walls round their new city and did much to succour them.

Nevertheless, Kos went over to Sparta in 409. This was part of a move that had begun in 412, when Kos and Rhodes together decided that alliance with Sparta would be more in their interests. Kos soon went back to the Athenian side, but in 405, when Lysander ravaged the Athenian fleet at Aegospotamoi, it was clear that Sparta was going to win the war and Kos joined it. Lysander abolished the island's democratic system and replaced it with a decarchy.

The Medical Tradition

Before the appearance of Hippocrates, patients on Kos - as throughout Greece - invoked and sacrificed to Asklepios, the god of medicine. The physicians who provided cures at the god's sanctuaries were called Asklepiades. There had been famous doctors from the island before, notably Nevros, Apollonidis (physician to King Ataxerxes), Hippocrates' own father (and teacher) Gnosidicos, and Herodicos or Prodicos, another of his mentors.

Hippocrates

Before proceeding with our account of the island's history, we should stop for a little to look at the personality and achievements of Hippocrates, the greatest physician of antiquity, who was born on Kos in 460 BC.

Hippocrates was the greatest of the ancient Asclepiades (physicians): he introduced the systematic classification of medicine and, according to Galen, was the first person to treat sickness in anything resembling a methodical manner. That is wr y even today he is called the father of medicine. Many ancient authors, including Eratosthenes, Pherecydes, Areios, Histomachus, Andreas and Soranos or Kos, wrote about Hippocrates and his work, and the later biographies of him which have survived - of Soranos of Ephesus, of Soudas or Souidas (in his Lexicon) and of the Byzantine Tzetzis - rely upon this early testimony.

On his father's side, Hippocrates was an 18th or 19th generation descendant of Asklepios, while on the side of his mother Phaenarete (or Praxithea) he was a 20th generation descendant of Herakles himself. Apart from medicine, he studied philosophy under Democritus and rhetoric with the sophist Gorgias and the orator Leontius. He studied at the Asklepeion of Kos and that of Ionia, and he had access to the papyri which Heraclitus had dedicated to the Asklepeio of Ephesus. In Miletus, he heard Anaxagoras lecture on matter, while in Samos and in Anaea on the coast of Asia Minor the general and philosopher Melissus told him of the theories of Pythagoras.

This great Koan scientist travelled in Macedonia, Thrace, Scythia, the islands of the Aegean, Smyrna, Athens, Egypt, Libya, the Peloponnese and Thessaly. In 430, he was in Delos; the Peloponnesian War had just broken out, and Athens had been struck by a terrible epidemic of cholera. Pericles summoned the wise physician to come to Athens, and he saved the city. The Athenians rewarded him in a number of ways: he was the second non-Athenian (after Heracles) to be admitted to the Eleusinian Mysteries, he was awarded a gold wreath, and they gave him the freedom of the city: he and his descendants were entitled to dine free of charge in the chief magistrates' quarters.

As a person, Hippocrates was modest and little interested in money. Tireless and always enthusiastic, he cured thousands of people and passed on his knowledge to the young. Only on two occasions did he refuse his services, both of them involving countries hostile to Greece: first the Illyrians and the Paeonians, and later the Persians, asked him to teach medicine in their lands, but he turned down their high fees and rich gifts.

Hippocrates spent the last years of his life in Larissa, where he died at the age of 104 (or 109, according to others) in the same year as Democritus. Soranus of Ephesus tells of seeing Hippocrates' tomb in the 2nd century AD, and much later writers, too, claimed to have visited it. Anthimos Gazis, for instance, contended in his Hellenic Library (1807) that "his tomb is extant even today". He said that he himself had seen it "by the roadside" among a number of Turkish graves. He also saw that there was an inscription on it, but was afraid to copy it because the Turks had gathered round him in a threatening manner.

Aristotelis P. Kouzis, Academician and university professor, wrote the following passage: *"Later, in March 1897, Dr S. Samartzidis of Larissa wrote of the tomb of Hippocrates, adding that in 1826, after a flood, a villager disovered a larnax some ten minutes away from the town of Larissa to the east of the road leading from Larissa to Turnavo, on the border between the villages of Yannouli and Kissaio. T. Andreadis and I. Economidis, scholars of Larissa, hastened to examine it. Digging down, they came upon a plaque inscribed quite clearly with the name of Hippocrates, but they were afraid to go any further. However, they begged a Turkish bey who was a protector of Christians to look after the plaque, and this was done, although the other things found in the larnax were stolen. When the bey died, Samartzidis saw the plaque in his house and copied the inscription, which he published in the periodical Iatriki Melissa (vol. 4, pp. 534, 6), and he also found the larnax."*

In his book on Kos, the tourist guide Georgios C. Soultanos gives the half-erased words of that inscription, which reads as follows:

.........ΙΠΠΟΚΡΑΤ...........ΚΩ...........
ΑΓΛΑΟΦ..........ΣΩΜΑ............ ΠΟΛΕΙ...
ΜΕΤΕΛΕΣΦ..........ΑΓΑΘΗ...........ΑΡ Ε..........
ΕΝΕΚΑ........ΧΡΗΣΤΕ........ΧΑΙΡΕ........

We have no idea what happened to the larnax and the inscription since that time. Hippocrates was a prolific writer of the greatest importance. Of all his works, 57 have survived, and they can be classified as general, anatomical and physiological, dietetic, pathological, prognostic, relating to special knowledge, therapeutic, surgical, ophthalmological, obstetrical and gynaecological, paediatric and miscellaneous. These works, together with the others that have not come down to us and Hippocrates' famous oath, were read by other doctors for many centuries and did much to convey the spirit and knowledge of Hippocrates.

Among other famous Koan doctors of antiquity (all of them, directly or indirectly, pupils of Hippocrates) were his sons Thessalos and

1. Ὄμνυμι Ἀπόλλωνα ἰητρόν καί Ἀσκληπιόν καί Ὑγείαν καί Πανάκειαν καί Θεούς πάντας τε καί πάσας ἵστορας ποιεύμενος, ἐπιτελέα ποιήσειν κατά δύναμιν καί κρίσιν ἐμήν ὅρκον τόνδε καί ξυγγραφήν τήνδε.

2. Ἡγήσασαι μέν τόν διδάξαντά με τήν τέχνην ταύτην ἴσα γενέτησιν ἐμοῖσι, καί βίου κοινώσασθαι καί χρεῶν χρηΐζοντι μετάδοσιν ποιήσασθαι καί γένος τό ἐξ αὐτοῦ ἀδελφεοῖς ἴσον ἐπικρινέειν ἄρρεσι, καί διδάξειν τήν τέχνην ταύτην, ἤν χρηΐζουσι μανθάνειν, ἄνευ μισθοῦ καί ξυγγραφῆς.

3. Παραγγελίης τε καί ἀκροήσιος καί τῆς λοιπῆς ἁπάσης μαθήσιος μετάδοσιν ποιήσασθαι υἱοῖσι τε ἐμοῖσι καί τοῖσι τοῦ ἐμέ διδάξαντος καί μαθηταῖσι συγγεγραμμένοις τε καί ὡρκισμένοις νόμῳ ἰητρικῷ, ἄλλῳ δέ οὐδενί.

4. Διαιτήμασί τε χρήσομαι ἐπ' ὠφελείῃ καμνόντων κατά δύναμιν καί κρίσιν ἐμήν, ἐπί δηλήσει δέ καί ἀδικίῃ εἴρξειν.

5. Οὐ δώσω δέ οὐδέ φάρμακον οὐδενί αἰτηθείς θανάσιμον, οὐδέ ὑφηγήσομαι ξυμβουλίην τοιήνδε· ὁμοίως δέ οὐδέ γυναικί πεσσόν φθόριον δώσω.

6. Ἁγνῶς δέ καί ὁσίως διατηρήσω βίον τον ἐμόν καί τέχνης τήν ἐμήν.

7. Οὐ τεμέω δέ οὐδέ μήν λιθιῶντας, ἐκχωρήσω δέ ἐργάτησιν ἀνδράσιν πρήξιος τῆσδε.

8. Ἐς οἰκίας δέ ὁκόσας ἄν ἐσίω, ἐσελεύσομαι ἐπ ὠφελείῃ καμνόντων, ἐκτός ἐών πάσης ἀδικίης ἑκουσίης καί φθορίης τῆ τε ἄλλης καί ἀφροδισίων ἔργων ἐπί τε γυναικείων σωμάτων καί ἀνδρείων, ἐλευθέρων τε καί δούλων.

9. Ἅ δ' ἄν ἐν θεραπείῃ ἤ ἴδω ἠ ἀκούσω, ἤ καί ἄνευ θεραπείης κατά βίον ἀνθρώπων, ἅ μή χρή ποτε ἐκλαλέεσθαι ἔξω, σιγήσομαι, ἄρρητα ἡγεύμενος εἶναι τά τοιαῦτα.

10. Ὅρκον μέν οὖν μοι τόνδε ἐπιτελέα ποιέοντι καί μή ξυγχέοντι εἴη ἐπαύρασθαι καί βίου καί τέχνης, δοξαζομένῳ παρά πᾶσιν ἀνθρώποις ἐς τόν ἀεί χρόνον· παραβαίνοντι δέ καί ἐπιορκέοντι, τἀναντία τουτέων.

The Hippocratic Oath

(Translation from ancient Greek: M. S. Kiapokas)

Dracon, his son-in-law Polybus, Praxagoras, Philinus, Critodemus (physician to Alexander the Great), Dracon the second, Hippocrates the fifth (physician to Roxane), Dexippus (physician to Mausolus), Erasistratus (physician to the court of the Seleucids), Nicas, Xenophon of Stertes (physician to the Emperor Claudius), Antipater Dioscourides (physician at Alassarna) and Nasander Anesipus (a pupil of the former). Hippocrates' son Dracon, who was also a doctor, is associated with a medieval myth about the island, which describes him and the sacred snake as figures of evil around the plane tree.

1. I swear by the physician Apollo and by Asklepios and by Hygeia and by Panacea and by all the gods and goddesses, who shall be my witnesses, that I shall fulfil this my oath and contract with all my power and judgement.

2. I will look upon him who shall have taught me this Art even as one of my parents. I will share my substance with him, and I will supply his necessities, if he be in need: I will regard his offspring even as my own brethren, and I will teach them this Art, if they would learn it, without fee or covenant.

3. I will impart this Art by precept, by lecture and by every mode of teaching, not only to my own sons but to those of him who has taught me, and to disciples bound by covenant and oath, accorduig to the Law of Medicine.

4. The regimen I adopt shall be for the benefit of my patients according to my ability and judgement, and not for their hurt or for any wrong.

5. I will give no deadly drug to any, though it be asked of me, nor will I counsel such, and especially I will not aid a woman to procure abortion.

6. I will keep my life and my Art pure and clean.

7. I will not engage in surgery upon those who suffer from stones, but will leave this task to those who are experienced.

8. Whatever house I enter, there will I go for the benefit of the sick, refraining from all wrongdoing or corruption, and especially from any act of seduction, of male or female, of slave or free.

9. Whatsoever things I see or hear concerning the life of men, in my attendance on the sick or even apart therefrom, which ought not to be noised abroad, I will keep silence thereon, counting such things to be as sacred secrets.

10. As long as I will keep this my oath, and as long as I will not violate it, may I be successful in my life and Art, and may I always have a good name among men, but if I infringe this oath and become an oath-breaker, may my fate be contrary.

The Fourth Century BC

After this digression on Hippocrates and the history of medicine on Kos, let us return to the events of the 4th century BC.

In 394, the Athenian admiral Conon defeated the navy of Sparta at Cnidus. Kos became an ally of Athens once more, and in 378 (or 377) joined the Second Athenian League, which was a federation of some 75 city-states.

Nonetheless, disputes continued on the island between the oligarchic party (who supported Sparta) and the democrats (who favoured Athens).

A serious clash in 366, which for a time appeared to be heading in the direction of civil war, was only averted by the need to organise the new capital of the island on a systematic basis. Located in the north-east of Kos, on the same site as the modern capital, this city needed new walls, a man-made harbour and other construction projects. This site had, of course, been occupied since very early times, and we have already seen that the remnants of a Mycenean settlement have been found there.

The other cities on the island agreed to be politically subject to the new town, and this proved to be a fruitful decision: thanks to its situation and its proximity to the Asklepion, Kos was soon able to build up a shipping and trade network which ushered in a fresh period of prosperity for the island as a whole.

At this time, the population of Kos was reported to be 160,000. The advances made in commerce were accompanied by progress in the arts and letters, and, as one would have expected, this prosperity and well-being provoked the envy of the monarchic regime in neighbouring Halicarnassus.

In 357 and 356 Kos and certain other former Athenian allies turned against Athens, at the instigation of King Mausolus of Halicarnassus and his wife and sister Artemisia the Younger. On Kos itself, the oligarchic party was behind this move, lured by gifts and promises from the court at Halicarnassus. In 355, Kos and the other renegades managed to split the Athenian League into two.

For some years after this, Kos was a possession of Halicarnassus. Democracy was abolished, and a military regime installed. The population dwindled, development ceased, many of the schools were forced to close and the leading teachers and artists chose to leave the island.

In 333, Alexander the Great's general Ptolemy managed to overcome the kingdom of Karia and captured Halicarnassus. The Koans hastened to seek an alliance with the Macedonians.

After the death of Alexander the Great in 323, his successors threw themselves into disputes and fighting. Kos sided with Ptolemy, now ruler of Egypt. Indeed, Ptolemy's son and heir, Ptolemy Philadelphus, was born on Kos in 309.

This forged even closer bonds between Kos and Alexandria, capital of the Ptolemies. As a result, the island was able to flourish once more, in commerce as well as in the arts. Many ancient writers tell us that at this time Kos exported considerable quantities of wine, olive oil, silk and woven goods.

Another Century of Prosperity

The strife and competition between the successors of Alexander the Great continued, however, and Kos came under a series of rulers. It chose always to side with the most powerful figure of the hour, and so its allegiance switched from Antigonus to Ptolemy and then back to Antigonus, returning once more to Ptolemy.

Progress, however, continued. In the 3rd century BC Kos occupied a position of distinction among the other Aegean islands, thanks to its wealth and the power of its fleet. The islanders seem to have played their political game cleverly, since apart from their links with the 'great powers' of the age they also kept up their bonds with progressive neighbouring islands such as Rhodes.

A marble inscription discovered in 1907 by the local archaeologist Iakovos Zaraftis tells us that Kos had formed a federation with the Kalydnes islands (Leros and Kalymnos), and that an oath of loyalty to the democratic system of government had been introduced.

In 220 BC the Koans joined their allies of Rhodes among the belligerents in the Second Macedonian War. But the Macedonians defeated the Rhodian and Koan fleet and forced it back to seek shelter in Kos harbour. Shortly afterwards, a fleet of ships from Ierapydna (modern Ierapetra) in Crete threatened the island's capital. The islanders rallied round and fought bravely at Cape Laceter (modern Cape Gourniatis, between Kardamaina and Kefalos), defeating the Cretan fleet and taking many prisoners. Another part of the fleet from Ierapydna had been making preparations to attack Halicarnassus, threatening the temple of Apollo there, but the Koans, under their admiral Nicostratus, managed to beat off this assault, too.

In the meantime, the power of the Romans had begun to grow and menace the Greek world. The Greek cities and the states ruled by Alexander's successors had worn themselves out in ceaseless squabbling. All the former 'great powers' of Greece and the Aegean were in decline.

Kos, together with Rhodes and Athens, quickly went over to the Roman side, in the belief that Rome would help them deal with the expansionist plans of Philip V of Macedon.

Roman Rule

Like the rest of the Greek cities, Kos failed to appreciate the true dimensions of the Roman threat. It totally underestimated the capacity and stamina of this new and warlike force that had arisen in the West. When they came face to face with the Roman legions and the powerful fleet, it was far too late to regroup their own forces and defend themselves with any hope of success.

In 197, Kos sided with the Romans, Attalus, King of Pergamum, and the Rhodians against Philip V of Macedon. Their united forces managed to defeat the hard-headed Macedonian at Cynoscephalae, and after this Kos decided to accept the 'protection' of Rome while at the same time maintaining its bonds with Rhodes and some other islands in the vicinity.

In 171, Kos took part in the Third Macedonian War, once more siding with Rhodes against Macedon.

Delos was declared a free port in 166, and this dealt the economy of Rhodes a serious blow. Kos was not so badly hit, perhaps because it was further away and had also kept up its relations with Egypt and Asia Minor.

Even in these difficult circumstances, Kos was capable of making progress. And despite the danger now apparent in the West, the island emerged once more as an important economic centre where the interests and wealth of numerous areas converged. At this time it was an important centre for banking.

Mithridates, King of Pont, captured Kos in 88 BC. Shortly before, he had defeated the Romans and occupied almost all of Asia Minor, ordering the slaughter of 80,000 Romans - or 150,000, according to other sources. Some of these people managed to take refuge in Kos and Rhodes, where they were welcomed. This enraged Mithridates, who attacked both islands. Rhodes, which was better fortified, managed to beat him off, and so he vented all his ire on Kos.

As far back as 102 BC, Cleopatra, consort of Ptolemy Evergetes, had left her grandson Alexander (later Ptolemy VIII) on Kos for safe-keeping, and had entrusted a large part of her fortune (and her will) to the Asklepeion. Mithridates took Alexander hostage and, scorning the sanctity and sanctuary of the shrine, seized Cleopatra's treasures and the savings of Jewish bankers which were also kept there, making off with an enormous sum of money.

To avenge their losses, Kos and Rhodes sent large numbers of ships to join the Roman fleet, in return for which Rome granted them various privileges.

In the meantime, the Roman Empire was steadily expanding, and Kos continued to be allied with it. Now the benefits were beginning to show, as the geographical position of the island, the quality of its produce and the renown of its Asklepion paid dividends.

In 82 BC the Romans finally rid Kos of the menace of Mithridates. The emperor Antony promulgated a law granting Roman citizenship to the islanders, the tetrarch Herod spent some time there in 32 BC, and the emperor Tiberius gave the Asklepion the right to function as a sanctuary.

Kos now became part of the Eastern Eparchy of the Roman Empire. Although the islanders had managed to secure various privileges, they were effectively under cold and calculating occupation. In order to justify their looting of the island's art treasures, the Romans deducted sizeable sums from the annual taxes they had introduced. On the other hand, they demanded that temples be erected to the deified Roman emperors, and imposed their own institutions.

In 5 or 6 BC the island was badly hit by an earthquake, and fresh destruction was caused by another in AD 142.

In the intervening period, Christianity began to make headway on the island.

St Paul called there on one of his missionary voyages. Although the Romans persecuted the Christian converts, quite a number of islanders went over to the new religion. To begin with, they were forced to worship in secrecy, but after the signing of the Edict of Milan in 313 they were free to practise their religion in public.

The Byzantine Period

After 330, when Constantine the Great moved the capital of the eastern Roman empire to Constantinople and founded the Byzantine Empire, Kos belonged to the theme (administrative district) of the Dodecanese.

Kos continued to be a profoundly Christian island, and countless churches in the basilica style of the age were crowded with enthusiastic congregations. Such churches, or their ruins, can still be seen all over the island today.

Interior of a Byzantine church.

All the coastal regions of the Byzantine Empire were subject to constant pirate raids. Given its geographical position and the wealth for which it was renowned, Kos repeatedly attracted the attention of freebooters hungry for loot.

In around 467 the Vandals sacked the island and caused great damage. In about 500 a fresh disaster occurred with the arrival of a horde of Visigoths under Alarichos. Then there were raids by Slavs and Arabs, which wrought more havoc.

The foundations of the houses in the Koumbourno quarter and at Psalidi show that in some early period the ground subsided by a metre or so. This occurred in 554, when one of the worst earthquakes in the island's history hit Kos and levelled the town, the villages and the Asklepion.

However, the Koans reacted as dynamically as they had always done after every human or natural disaster, and soon rebuilt their houses and amassed more wealth.

This, of course, served only to attract the attention of the pirates once more, and there were raids by the Saracens in 612 and shortly afterwards by a small group of Normans.

Western Rule

The Crusaders (of various nationalities: Venetians, French, Germans, etc.) first appeared in the East around 1160. On the pretext of religious causes, they conducted campaigns of looting and robbery.

In 1204, the islands of the Aegean, including Kos, mainland Greece and Byzantium itself fell to the Crusaders, known in Greece as 'the Franks'. Three-eighths of the Empire, including the islands, fell to the lot of Venice. Leo Gavalas became governor of the islands, and declared himself independent prince of Rhodes and Kos. As a result, Kos came under an unusual form of Western rule for a number of years.

The Byzantine Emperor Michael Palaeologus managed to recapture Byzantium and drive out the Western conquerors of Kos, but the Empire was clearly in decline and the situation continued to be unstable.

Palaeologus had been obliged to seek the help of Genoese admirals, and he had to reward them for their efforts. The ambitious and mercenary Genoese soon fell to quarrelling over their new lands, seeking ever-greater profits. And as soon as their attention was attracted elsewhere, there were pirates lying in wait to snatch their prey. Around 1312 Kos fell victim to repeated attacks by Catalans and Moors.

In 1309, the Genoese masters of the area sold Kos and their other lands to Foulques de Villaret, Grand Master of the Order of the Knights of St John. The Knights arrived in Kos in 1314 or 1315, and stayed for 220 years.

In 1347 the island was hit by an epidemic which carried off much of the population. In the meantime, the threat posed by the pirates

Views from the Venetian castle and the coat-of-arms.

from Europe or Asia had been magnified by the appearance of the Turks, who had begun to capture the islands off the Asia Minor coast. The Knights, with the help of local people and reinforcements from Rhodes, managed to drive off repeated Turkish attacks, even though the Turks threw thousands of men and many hundreds of ships into the battle.

Ottoman Rule

What the Koans had suffered at the hands of the Knights and the pirates was nothing compared to the torments they

would undergo during Ottoman rule. In 1523, Sultan Suleyman, after occupying Rhodes, took Kos as well.

The Knights of St John had reached an understanding with him - to the benefit of both sides - and so they were able to leave the island without many losses and taking a good part of their wealth with them. Persecution, oppression and humiliation of the Greek population began at once.

The Turkish conquerors behaved in the most barbaric of manners, imposing levies of Christian children, ordering massacres and frightful tortures on an everyday basis and constantly stepping up their economic demands. Apart from milking the island dry, their aim was also to convert its Christian population to Islam. Many Koans met their ends as a result of their loyalty to their faith. Among them was the martyr Ioannis the Boatswain, who was burned alive by the Turks on 8 April 1669.

In 1603, the Knights of St John attempted to recapture Kos, but failed. All they succeeded in doing was to loot the island and carry off some hundreds of its women, who were sold in the slave markets of Tunis. Kos was raided by Spanish and Moorish corsairs in 1601, 1603 and 1610.

Yet despite their hardships and the persecution to which they were subjected, the Koans retained their national pride intact. They found ways of taking part in all the struggles of the enslaved Greek nation for freedom. During the Russo-Turkish wars of the 18th century, frequent rebellions broke out on the island. Many islanders joined the 'Philike Etaireia', the 'society of friends' which organised the Greek War of Independence, and worked within its ranks.

When the War of Independence began, Kos of course sided with the other Greeks. The Turks, receiving information that the Koans were supplying the revolution with men and materials, hanged 92 of the island's leading citizens from Hippocrates' plane tree on 6 June 1821, and executed 26 more at Kako Prinari.

In later years, the Koans were often saved from the frenzied revenge of their Turkish masters by the intervention of respected church leaders or the consuls of the foreign powers.

Italian Rule

On 7 May 1912, after centuries of brutal Turkish rule, Italy landed men on Kos from her fleet and occupied the island, stating that her role was that of liberator. The islanders welcomed the Italians enthusiastically, in the belief that they would only stay for a short while and that they were a guarantee of incorporation of the Dodecanese into free Greece.

On 20 December 1912, the entire population of Kos, under the leadership of the bishop and the elders of the community, gathered to approve a petition which was dispatched to the great powers of the day. This stated that the Koans had maintained their Greek nationality unalloyed for centuries, that they rejected any prospect of restoration of Turkish rule, and that they wished to be united with the rest of Greece as soon as possible.

The Italian declaration that their presence on the island was merely temporary and that they would respect the religious, educational and administrative rights of the islanders turned out to be misleading. The other powers were unwilling to step in and ensure that the Greeks were given their rights. Thus a period of Italian occupation began in Kos as on the other islands of the Dodecanese. Conditions were tolerable for the Greek population in the first years, but when Fascism came to power in Italy, the governors of the island began to act in a more oppressive manner towards the Greeks. The occupation and the terrible earthquake of 1933 combined to force large portions of the population of the upland villages to emigrate. The earthquake led to the formation of new villages such as Zipari and Mastihari, which have grown rapidly, especially in recent years.

Land in the most fertile parts of Kos was confiscated (that is, acquired by compulsory purchase for negligible compensation) and settlers from southern Italy were installed there. Greek schools were closed, and only Italian schools functioned. There was a ban on the ordination of Orthodox priests, and so many town parishes and villages were left without religious functionaries.

As soon as Italy declared war on Greece in 1940, many islanders were arrested and taken to a concentration camp on Rhodes, where they spent a considerable period of time living in appalling conditions with detainees from all over the Dodecanese. Two years before this, the Italians had caused a cultural catastrophe: on the orders of the governor, thirty ancient mosaics and statues were removed from Kos and taken to Rhodes. The mosaics were used to decorate the floors in the Palace of the Knights, while nine of the statues still stand in the courtyard of that building, which the Italians had restored.

Unification at last

When Italy capitulated in 1943, the Germans took over the occupation of Kos and a fresh period of deprivation and famine began for the islanders.

Barbarities started even in the first days under the new regime. The Germans had no hesitation in hanging patriots on the mere suspicion of membership of the resistance movement. The Koans had to do forced labour for the Germans, who totally ruined the island's stock-breeding and its entire economy. Hangings of Greeks continued to take place until the last few days before liberation, and the Germans also executed scores of Italian officers, of all ranks, for being insufficiently pro-German.

During the German occupation, a considerable amount of damage was caused by bombing raids.

Some of the island's Greeks fled to the Middle East, while many of the Turks of Kos moved secretly across to Asia Minor. The Jews of the island were arrested, and sent to concentration camps in Germany.

On 9 May 1945, Kos was occupied by British troops acting on behalf of the Allied powers. The difficult task of rebuilding the island's economy began. Since Greek Kos was now being created once more, it was only natural that many of the island's Turks left for Asia Minor.

Liberation in 1946 brought back to Kos some of the islanders who had left at earlier times.

At last unification with Greece, for which the Koans had longed for so many years, took place. The Greek flag was raised over Kos on 7 March 1948, and was greeted by the islanders - now forever liberated - with unrestrained enthusiasm. However, the island continued to have an acute demographic problem. Emigration to America and Australia during the Fifties caused the population to shrink, and the census of 1971 revealed that it had fallen by over 2,000 by comparison with the census of 1947 (18,545).

The official census of 1981 put the population at the higher figure of 20,350, an impressive rise which reflects the island's development for tourism and the return of many of those who had emigrated to set up small (family-sized) hotel units in the main town and the chief tourist resorts. Today the population has reached a figure of around 24,000.

CULTURE & TRADITION

Kos impresses the visitor from the first moment that he sees it, whilst still on the boat. A little later, as he wanders around the spaces of historical and cultural memory, he finds himself in the shade of Hippocrates' plane tree, among the imposing buildings dating from the Ottoman period and that of the Italian occupation of the island. Here he will admire the ancient tree and recalls the father of medicine, Hippocrates. Descending in his car from Antimacheia for the city, the picture is quite different. A sunny and open countryside with haystacks in the plains, which stretch down as far as the sea. From the opposite side of Mesaria, reaching as far as the foothills of Mt Dikios, there is a plain with small hills, vines and vegetable gardens, producing mainly tomatoes and also a few other garden vegetables, reminders of the island's rich produce of water and honey melons. Tobacco and sesame, the main produce of the island's residents in the first post-war years, have now become history, just as the rich produce in tomatoes, which once had seven tomato puree factories, is almost history.

The great growth in tourism means that Kos's recent past, a past of farming and live-stock rearing, is today almost over. The social changes that followed also explain that change which has taken place in the social and economic structure of Kos from a rural to an urban-tourist society. The demographic changes, especially the settlement on the island of populations from other parts of Greece and even from abroad, in order to serve the increased needs of the tourist industry, have changed the social structure of the local population. A population which was made up primarily of indigenous Koans and a few Muslims, who were employed in live-stock rearing.

A multi-cultural population mix of great interest is being invited to take on a new role in the history of the island. It is being invited to go forward hand-in-hand with tradition, customs and practices and to guide the island to a new reality. In a place which is aware of its cultural roots, any change can be strong and stable only if it involves a creative absorption of outside elements. This should always be a matter of partnership and never a matter of something new coming to predominate or something old being done away with.

This is why Kos inspires wonder. Because it knows how to evolve.

People and Occupations

As with most of the residents of the Greek islands, the Koans are friendly and peace-loving people. Many of them impress with their diligence and hospitality. In the villages especially, the spirit of helping each other and cooperation that was prevalent during the years of subjugation to foreign rule (prior to 1948) is still strong. Despite the great growth of tourism, the desire to be helpful, the sense of honour and humanity, have not abandoned the Koans.

Kos is a rich island and the residents who make their living from it do not have especial problems. Kos is one of the most fertile islands of the Aegean and the phrase "whoever Kos has raised, he is not an Egyptian" was popular in antiquity. For this reason, until the 1960s most of the residents, about four-fifths, were involved in farming and live-stock raising. Today around half of the working population works in hotels and the tourist industry. There are 260 hotels, with 6,500 three-person rooms containing around 66,000 beds, which employ 7,800 members of staff (1999 figures) for five to seven months of the year.

One section of the population (around 1/5) is employed in farming and live-stock raising. There are also areas of flat land in Kos where garden vegetables, such as tomatoes, water and honey melons, courgettes, aubergines, okra, beans, lettuce, etc. are watered and grown. There are 16 greenhouses which provide the local market with early garden produce. The provision of grants has resulted in an increase in olive growers (2000) in the past few years. The olive orchards cover an area of 25,000 square metres with a total of 650,000 trees. There are also three modern olive presses. The island also produces cereals, wheat, barley, oats and corn. The live-stock farmers grow clover, vetch and other plants with which to graze their animals.

There is also a distillery on Kos, two dairy-produce factories, two fizzy drinks plants, a tannery and several small industries which employ several dozen workers.

Local cuisine

One of the foods prepared by the housewives of Kos are the 'pittaridia.' These are made of dough prepared with flour and water, just like the noodles known as 'hilopites.' After kneading they roll it with the 'pittarido-stick,' cut the dough into long pieces, sprinkle it with butter and myzithra cheese and cook it in meat stock. It is usually served on the eve of a wedding.

Another local dish is the 'pasa-makarona,' a type of pasticcio dish, i.e. with layers of mince, cheese and béchamel sauce. This particular dish is made with home-made filo pastry leaves, the dough of which is prepared with eggs. The filling is made with pork mince and fresh myzithra cheese. Before being cooked the pasa-makarona is sprinkled with meat stock and milk. It is usually eaten during the Easter carnival.

The local cheeses of Kos are put into the 'krasi' (wine) or the 'tyria' (cheese), i.e. in the wine sediment. These red cheeses, are they call them, are very tasty and make delicious cheese pies and other such dishes.

At the fairs of Kos they often serve, in addition to the other dishes, 'yiaprakia,' i.e. dolmades wrapped with vine leaves.

In the western villages of Kos, moreover, they make 'marmarites.' These are made from a special gruel which is cooked in individual portions in pre-heated marble dishes. They dip them in beaten egg, fry them in pork fat, and drench then with grape-juice syrup. Marmarites are usually eaten during Epiphany.

Another dish that many Kos housewives still make in the week before Lent is the 'katimeria.' These are made with home-made filo pastry leaves cut into square or round pieces and which are then filled with myzithra and egg, fried and then drenched with syrup or honey.

One of the sweets that the housewives of Kos make, especially at Christmas and New Year, are 'sarmousades.' These are made with either walnuts or almonds that are wrapped in home-made filo leaves and sliced into a diamond-shaped portions, like a baklava. They are cooked in a large pan.

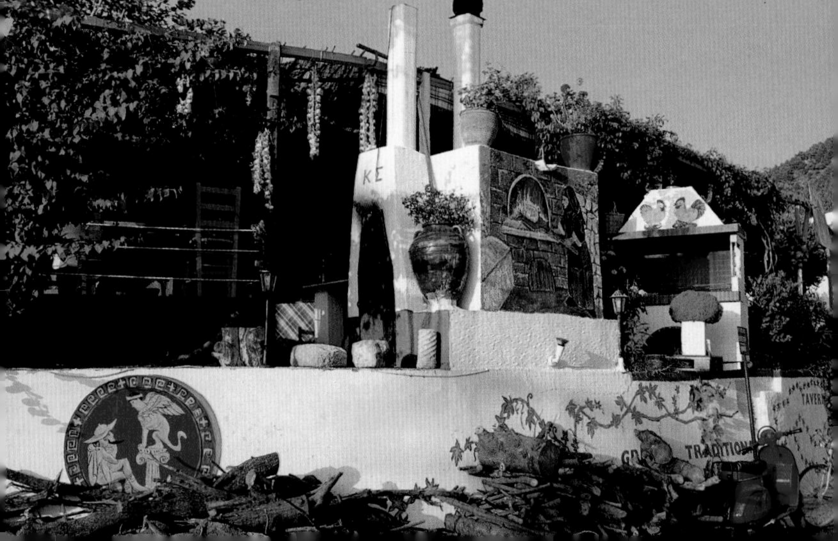

Customs and Tradition

The island's residents still maintain many of the old customs. Typical is the **custom of 5th September**: before sunset, the housewives take two wreaths, an old and a new one, of pomegranates, grapes, garlic, an olive branch, and leaves from the plane-tree of Hippocrates down to the sea. They throw the old wreath into the sea and place the new one at the edge of the water, so that it will be lapped by forty waves. Holding the new wreath, 'the beginning of the year,' as it is called, and a pannikin with sea water and pebbles, they pass by the plane-tree of Hippocrates, where they clasp its trunk in order to take strength, weight and years from its years. When they return home they hang the wreath on the iconostasis and sprinkle the rainwater with the pebbles in the corner of the house to protect against the dangers of wagging tongues.

The honey festival.

Another custom which is maintained by some farmers is the **'swine-slaughter,'** which takes place in October or November. Relatives and friends are invited and, after the slaughter and portioning out of the pig, delicacies are cooked, barrels of wine are opened and a party follows. This custom has recently been bolstered by local associations, who invite many guests.

On 30 November, the feast of Saint Andrew, or Ayios Andreas, many housewives prepare **'akoumia,'** that is 'loukoumades' (a kind of doughnut), which they send to friends and relatives. On 4 December, the feast of Ayia, or Saint, Barbara, they make **'varvara'** with cooked wheat, tahini, currants, sesame, walnuts, pomegranates, cinnamon and other spices. In this way they honour Ayia Barbara, who is considered to protect children from smallpox.

Carols celebrating Christmas, New Year and the Epiphany are still sung by small children in the homes or by groups of schoolchildren or youngsters with musical instruments in the streets. On the day of the Epiphany, large crowds of people congregate in the churches and on the beaches during the asperges and the throwing of the cross into the sea.

The **'Apokries,'** the carnival celebrations during which meat is eaten just before Lent, are celebrated with gatherings in the houses of relatives, meals and carnival songs. For the musical instrument they usually use a round, metal dish called a 'lingeri' or a 'vatselli.' Children and youths dress up as 'kamouzelles,' i.e. in masquerade, and they go around the houses and cafes teasing each other and playing out comic sketches. In the villages they prepare the 'kokkala,' the skull of a donkey. They dress it in a sheepskin, hang bells from it, place it on a cane and pass a rope through it so that its jaws open and close. It is held up by someone who is masked and wrapped in a rug, and he and his friends take the 'kokkala' around the houses.

On the **Saturday of Lazarus** many housewives prepare the 'lazarakia': using a special dough, they prepare long and narrow small breads, fill them with ground currants, sesame and aromatic spices. They shape them into the figure of a shrouded man, just as Lazarus is represented, stick two cloves in as eyes and cook the breads so that the whole family can eat them during Easter Week when they are fasting.

The **feast of Ayios Georgios** (Saint George) on 23 April, is always celebrated with horse races at the Gate of Kos.

The **feast of Ayios Ioannis** (St John) on 24 June is accompanied by the custom of the fire ("of the torch," as they say) and the ivy. In the past few years, aside from in the gardens of the houses, the custom of the torch is also celebrated in the central square of Kos town by the local section of the Lykeio Ellinidon (Greek Girls' Lycee). Young and old jump over the flames of the fire. This is followed by local dances, watched by the many visitors to the island.

Traditional costume

The traditional men's costume of Kos features primarily the island breeches (vraka), either in black or blue, the shirt, the velvet 'yialeli,' i.e. sleeveless waistcoat which was cross-buttoned, and the 'zaka,' a short coat with sleeves that was not buttoned up at the front. In the winter, instead of the zaka, they wore the 'patatoukla,' a woollen coat with buttons. Around the waist they wore woollen belts with green or black embroidery. On holidays and feast days many men would wear white belts with stripes and fringes around their breeches. On their heads they wore a fez or a cap made of black velvet. Villagers had three types of shoe: the 'yemenia,' shoes made of local leather that covered the whole foot and with thick soles, which were worn when working; the 'jesmedes,' which reached up to the knees and were worn at celebrations; and the 'papadistika,' similar to today's shoes, which were worn mainly by the elderly.

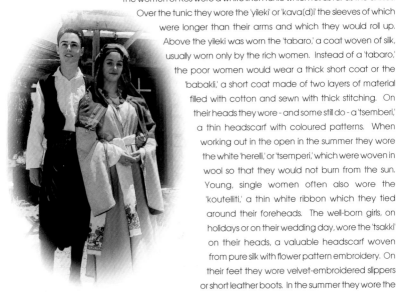

The women of Kos wore a white linen tunic which fell as far as the ankles. Over the tunic they wore the 'yileki' or 'kava(d)i' the sleeves of which were longer than their arms and which they would roll up. Above the yileki was worn the 'tabaro,' a coat woven of silk, usually worn only by the rich women. Instead of a 'tabaro,' the poor women would wear a thick short coat or the 'babakli,' a short coat made of two layers of material filled with cotton and sewn with thick stitching. On their heads they wore - and some still do - a 'tsemberi,' a thin headscarf with coloured patterns. When working out in the open in the summer they wore the white 'herelli,' or 'tsemperi,' which were woven in wool so that they would not burn from the sun. Young, single women often also wore the 'koutelliti,' a thin white ribbon which they tied around their foreheads. The well-born girls, on holidays or on their wedding day, wore the 'tsakki' on their heads, a valuable headscarf woven from pure silk with flower pattern embroidery. On their feet they wore velvet-embroidered slippers or short leather boots. In the summer they wore the

so-called 'wooden' sandals with wooden soles. Today these costumes are no longer worn except on parades, traditional festivals and certain cultural events, such as those that are organised by the Lykeio Ellinidon of Kos, which works with great devotion to keep the traditions alive.

Musical tradition

Kos has had a rich musical tradition from antiquity. In Hellenistic times, Kos produced 20 artists (singers, kithar players, flautists and harpists) alone, that is half of those from the Dodecanese as a whole. During the Byzantine era, religious music had a great influence on the musical tradition of the islands. The Franks (western Europeans) who occupied the Aegean after the Crusades brought new musical and poetic forms with them, such as rhyme, and musical instruments such as the violin. Frankish rhyme blended with the pure Greek element, the iambic fifteen-syllable metre, creating the mantinada, the improvised rhyming couplet, on Kos as well. During the Ottoman era the soulful aman songs were introduced to the islands. The musical tradition of the Dodecanese has creatively absorbed eastern elements and western influences, thus creating a rich and diverse musical tradition. The musical tradition of Kos also features in this broader context, and in the broader context of the Aegean as well.

On Kos the most impressive **musical instruments** that are still used today at weddings, fairs and other events are the violin, the lute and the lyre. Shepherds would make the tsabouna (a kind of bagpipe) and the piniauli using reeds, and played these instruments when grazing their sheep. The musicians today usually play old tunes, whilst on rare occasions they might add a melodic embellishment or new rhythms.

The island's **dances** have followed a similar tradition. One of the most common dances of Kos is the 'sianos,' from siganos, which means slow. It is a simple dance with seven steps during which the dancers, men and women, hold onto each other with their arms crossed and dance in a circle. Another dance with more figures and airs is the sousta, a variation on the Cretan dance of the same name, a fast-paced dance with small leaps. The ballo is also danced, dating to the period of Frankish rule, as is the syrtos dance from Constantinople and Rhodes, the kalamatianos, and many other dances.

The **songs** of Kos, as of the other Dodecanese islands, have a diverse subject matter: religion, social issues, history, the family, agriculture, the seasons, weddings, satire, proverbs, dirges, lullabies, and others. At many weddings even today, singers and lyricists sing special songs as the bride and groom are being dressed, as the bride and groom lead the dance (the siano), etc. Of those songs which do not accompany dances the 'Dyosmaraki' is typical, whilst the 'Melachrino' is a song for dance. Interesting variations of border songs are still preserved. Of the demotic songs which tell a tale, quite widespread are the 'stichoplakies' (lyric jokes) which tell of traditions, the émigrés, adventures, life's pleasant and unpleasant events.

Cultural events

Cultural events on the island are organised by many bodies, such as the Municipality of Kos Cultural Centre, the Provincial Cultural Committee, the Cultural Committees of the new municipalities of Dikaios and Herakleios and by cultural associations. The cultural associations which arrange activities are: the Filitas Cultural Circle of Koans; the Lykeio Ellinidon of Kos, the Theokritos Educational Association of Asfenidou; the Apelles Cultural Association of Pyli; the Proodos (Progress) Cultural Association of Antimacheia; the Argos Cultural Association of Kardamaina; the Cultural Association of Kefalos; the Conservation and Nature-lovers Association of Kos; the Kos Cinema Club, and others. Among the most impressive of the regular events that are organised are the lectures presented by figures from the arts and literature. Colloquia and conferences are organised on subjects relating to local culture. Contests are held in which the young can participate, with prizes being awarded.

There are choruses, theatre teams, and dance groups which organise public events. Diaries with themes from popular culture are published. Book fairs, featuring books on the Dodecanese and other subjects, take place. There are trips and guided tours to the archaeological sites. Open meetings to discuss the problems of young people are held. Events which help maintain traditional customs are organised. In the past few years some cultural associations, such as the Kos Cultural Centre, the Cultural Centre of the Koans, Filitas, the Provincial Cultural Committee of Kos and others, have published acclaimed works by Koan scholars on the history, culture and traditions of the island.

In the summer months the three municipalities organise cultural programmes: the Hippokrateia in Kos town, the Dikaia in the Municipality of Dikaios and the Herakleia in the Municipality of Herakleios. These programmes of events last for 8-10 weeks, with theatrical productions, concerts, traditional dances, art exhibitions, traditional festivals, events organised by Koans from abroad, etc. One event of especial importance is the reconstruction of the Hippocratic Oath, which takes place at the

Asklepion of Kos in the presence of many of the island's visitors: young women dressed in white costume and bearing baskets walk in a slow and rhythmic pattern down two groups (6+6) of the first tier or seats in the Asklepion, whilst in the middle three flautists dressed in chitons play a rhythmic piece of music. They are followed by a young man crowned with a wreath and carrying a parchment with the Hippocratic Oath written upon it. He is accompanied by two young women dressed in white. When they reach the second level, the basket-holders throw flowers over the altar of Asklepios and seat themselves around the altar. Here, in an evocative atmosphere, the young man crowned with the wreath reads out the Oath of Hippocrates.

Arts and letters

Thanks to Hippocrates, Kos is considered to be the cradle of medicine. Many celebrated doctors of antiquity studied at the school established by the founder of medicine. These include Praxagoras, the best anatomist of the 4th century BC; Dexippos, a distinguished doctor and student of Hippocrates; Kritodemos, a famous surgeon and the personal doctor of Alexander the Great; Kalippos, who saved the lives of many citizens at Aptera in Crete and was honoured with a golden crown; and Xenotimos, who was also honoured with a golden crown for saving many patients. Filinos, the founder of the empirical school of medicine (3rd century BC) was also from Kos. The island's medical tradition continued into the 1st century AD. Sertinius Xenophon, the personal doctor of the Emperor Tiberius Claudius (AD 41) was from Kos. During the island's acme in the 3rd century BC, the scholar and poet Philetas the Koan founded a philosophical school, from which many great figures graduated. These include Theocritus (whose father was from Kos), the greatest bucolic poet of antiquity, Herondas, the best writer of mimes in the Hellenistic period, and Ptolemy II, one of the most important Kings of Egypt, who was born in Kos in 309 BC.

Apelles (356-276 BC), one of the ancient world's greatest painters, lived in Kos for many years and it was here that he painted some of his celebrated works. His 'Aphrodite Rising from the Sea' was one of the best paintings to decorate the Asklepion of Kos, remaining there for three centuries until the Emperor Augustus took it back to Rome with him when he occupied Kos.

The art of the mosaic was highly developed in Kos. The halls of the Castle of Kos are decorated with some wonderful mosaics. One of the best, with representations of fish, is today on exhibit in the Museum of Kos.

Music is another of the arts which flourished in Kos. One of the island's most important musicians was Dioscurides the kithar player, who won first prize at the Asklepieia contest of 182 BC. Other distinguished musicians were the kithar player Theomnestos in the first century BC, who was known as a harp-player, Alexander the singer who lived in the 2nd century AD, etc.

Of the island's philosophers, two of the most important were Evimeros (340-260 BC) and Ariston, a peripatetic philosopher of the 2nd century BC. The most well-known Koan historians are Makareus, who wrote the "Koaka," and Sisyphus, who wrote about the Trojan war. The lived in the Hellenistic period, as did Xenokritos, a Koan scholar who is considered to be one of the most important commentators of the works of Hippocrates. There was also a school of astrology on Kos, founded by the Babylonian priest Berossos around 270 BC in order to spread the astrological learning of the Chaldeans.

The legislature of the Koans, moreover, was one of the best of the Hellenistic period and many of the laws of Kos were adopted by other cities. Koan judges were often invited by many other islands and cities to give their opinion on certain cases.

The education system of Kos was excellently organised. Aside from reading and writing and music, the Koans placed great emphasis on exercise and gymnastics. It is for this reason that many great athletes came from Kos, such as Xenombrotos, who won repeatedly in the horse-races at Olympia (380 BC), Xenodikos, also Olympic victor in the boys' boxing category (376 BC), Filinos the sprinter, who was victor for around ten years (268 BC), Isthmias, Pythias, Nemeas, and others. Among the many other distinguished athletes were Damokrates the wrestler, the victor in the Boeotian Games (190 BC) and Damoxenes the champion shot-putter.

Architecture

The architecture of the islands has also been effected by the development of tourism and above all by the erection of so many hotels. The sheer volume of building in the town and the tourist resorts is quite astounding. The architectural appearance of Kos town in the period after the earthquake, with its two-storey buildings with wooden doors and windows painted blue, has changed beyond recognition. Modern buildings have gone up in their place - to meet the needs of the present day, of course, but there is not a single breath of the past about them. Only the historic part of the town called Havouzia, behind the church of Ayia Paraskevi, has survived under a preservation order. Asfendiou, too, has been scheduled as an example of traditional architecture, and it conveys some memories of the lifestyle, occupations and vernacular architecture of Kos.

The houses were built with stone and mortar consisting of ordinary earth and a little lime. Door and window openings were flanked by delicate dressed stone pillars of the same height and width as the aperture.

Roofs had wooden beams topped with layers of cane. Over the canes were laid seaweed and pouolana, a kind of clay, and a further layer of patelia, a sort of shiny earth, provided the finishing touch.The roof would also have a chimney-pot. Houses were usually oriented south-east.

Many of the simple houses to be seen in the main town and country areas have kept this vernacular style of architecture or the style of interior decoration common for very many years.

KOS TOWN

The activities never stop in the bustling and brightly-lit port of Kos town, the centre of life and capital of the island..

LEGEND
1. Port
2. Polytechnic Square
3. Roman Forum
4. Town Hall - Customs House
5. Tourist Police
6. National Bank
7. Eleftherias Square
8. Defterdar Mosque
9. Archaeological Museum
10. Market
11. Ayia Paraskevi
12. Ancient Mosaics
13. Ancient Stadium
14. Constantine Palaeologos Square
15. Diagoras Square
16. Gymnasium (Xystos)
17. Ancient Hippodrome
18. Ancient Nymphaion
19. Ancient Odeion
20. Roman House
21. Long-distance bus station
22. Olympic Airways
23. Ionian Bank
24. Telecommunications (OT
25. Post Office
26. Taxi rank
27. Castle
28. The plane-tree of Hippocr
29. Hajji Hasan Mosque
30. Local Government Buildin
31. Ancient Agora
32. Hospital
33. Archbishopric
34. Hovercraft
35. 3rd September Square
36. Pisteos Bank
37. Agrotiki Bank
38. Port Authority
LAMBI
FILINOU
KRITIS
PORFYRIOU
P. GERMANOU
ANTIMACHOU
AKTI KOUNTOURIOTOU
AMERIKIS
IGIAS
AVEROF
THEMISTOKLEOUS
NEOMART. CHRISTOU
KANARI
Agios Pavlos
PAMFILON
NAVARINOU
SPETSON
ETHNIKIS ANTISTASSIS
PIXIOTON
YDRAS
SALAMINOS
MANDILARA
PSARON
PATAKOU
ALIKARNASOU
BOUBOULINAS
IRODOTOU
VEROPOULOU
NIKIFOROU
LOCHOU
IEROU
OMIROU
KYPROU
PINDOU
AKTI KOUN TOURIOTOU
FERAIOU
MEGALOU ALEXANDROU
31 MARTIOU
25th MARTIOU
DIAKOU
AL.
NAVKLIROU
IPPOK
ELEFTHERIOU VENIZELOU
TSALDARI
GALLIAS
MAKARIOU
KREKOUKI
KOLOKOTRONI
YPSILANTOU
DAMOCHAREOS
ZERVOU
KLEOVOULOU
IFESTOU
XANTHOU
THEOFRASTOU
MEG ALEXANDROU
CHRISTODOULOU
METSOVOU
ANT. IOANNIDI
VASILEOS PAVLOU
MEROPIDOS
KORITSASOULOU
AG. PAVLOU
APELOU
ARGYROKASTROU
PISANDROU
KLEOPATRAS
KAVAKOPOULOU
VIRONOS
SKEVOU
EGILION
ZARAFTOU
V. IPIROU
GRIGORIOU E'
TO ASKLIPIEION
EM. PAPPA
FINIK
N

The capital of Kos, which has the same name as the island, is one of the most beautiful towns of Greece today. Its population, according to the results of the most recent censuses, is around 16,000. The town of Kos has a planned modern layout, wide roads, a beautiful beach with a man-made harbour, rows of trees and gardens, the imposing Castle of the Knights, and many archaeological sites, in combination with buildings of different styles and eras. It also has modern hotels, restaurants, cafes, bars and clubs.

The combination of contemporary buildings with structures and remains that are representative of many other eras creates a particularly delightful atmosphere. The abundant vegetation, which at some points is even tropical, contributes greatly to the town's charm. Today's town has been built on an anti-earthquake design, after the catastrophic earthquake of 1933. From antiquity even, the capital has experienced, as has the whole of the island, many catastrophic earthquakes. Some call Kos 'the town of the bicycles' because so many journeys are made by bicycle. The connections with the villages of the island are, of course, made by coach or taxi.

The regular sea and air connections have greatly assisted in the growth of domestic and foreign tourism. Each year Kos attracts thousands of visitors from other countries and, especially in the summer, the presence of these tourists creates a particularly cosmopolitan environment.

The first point of reference for every visitor is the port. Here, life continues all day long. As soon as the last revelers in the restaurants and cafes have craled off to bed, life of a different sort begins. Fishermen and fish merchants come and go, and caiques sail in and out of the **harbour**. At 4 or 5 in the morning, there are even cargo ships to give a completely different picture to the harbour. Around the stalls in the fish market bustles a colourful crowd.

Steamers, fishing-boats and pleasure craft come and go, carrying people and mer-chandise.

Akti Koundourioti is the name of the street running along the waterfront; it has shops of all kinds, with signs in foreign languages, bars, restaurants and hotels.

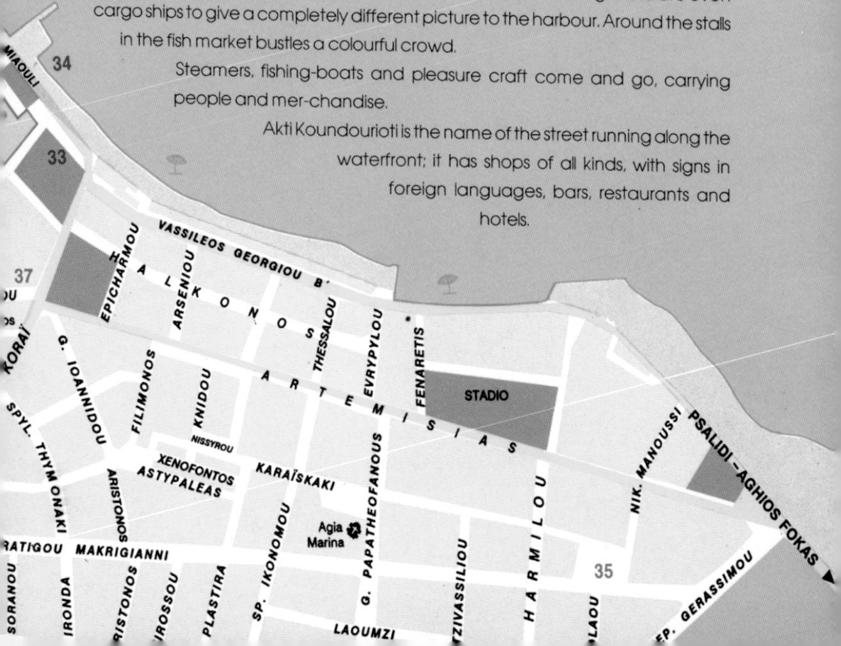

Eleftherias (Freedom) **Square** lies very near to the port. Shops, the market, the Museum, the Defterdar mosque, bustling crowds and endless comings and goings – that is Eleftherias Square, near the harbour. Around are alleyways with shops where one can spend a pleasant hour browsing, even if one has no particular intention of buying.

The Archaeological Museum of Kos is on the north side of the main Eleftherias Square, near the harbour, opposite the un-usual market building and the typically Turkish Defterdar Mosque (see page 68-71).

Akti Koundouriotou ends in Platanou Square. Here is the Castle of the Knights, the island's most imposing and impressive building. In front of the Castle's main entrance is the enormous plane tree with a diameter of some ten metres. This is the famous **plane tree of Hippocrates**, supposedly planted some 2,400 years ago by the great physician himself. According to the local traditions, it was here, under the welcom-ing shade of the branches of the tree, that Hippocrates taught many of his pupils. Another legend tells us that the ancient Koans set up a statue of their famous fellow islander Philetas (334-270 BC), a poet, beneath the tree.

Since the plane tree stands close to the harbour in an area that has been cool and shady since ancient times, much of the official life of Kos town has taken place here in many periods of its history. It may well be on this spot that St Paul spoke to the inhabitants of Kos and spread the word of Christianity, the new religion.

It was only natural that this aged and imposing tree should have become associated in the local mind with various myths and legends. It was seen as a tree of great power, and various customs - many of

1

2

3

Opposite: the plane-tree of Hippocrates and the Defterder mosque.

1. The church of Ayia Paraskevi.
2. The entrance to the Archaeological Museum.
3., 4 The Municipal Market.

ΘΕΜΙΣ

NIKITAS

Pellini

them still honoured on 1 September each year - are associated with it.

In Turkish times an ancient sarcophagus was placed next to the trunk of the tree, widely believed to be among the largest in Europe. A stream of water was diverted into the sarcophagus, thus creating the fountain of the Loggia Mosque. The mosque, which stands opposite, is a typical building of its type, with pieces of ancient monuments built into its walls. According to an inscription, work on the con-struction of the mosque and the fountain was begun in 1786 by Gazi Hasan Pasha.

After Platanou Square comes **Akti Miaouli,** which has an excellent sandy beach for swimming and sunbathing.The whole area is full of gardens, tree-lined avenues, and the buildings typical of the Italian period of occupation. The Local Government building, with its clock, the Archbishopric with the Archbishop's residence, the gates in the Venetian walls, the plane trees and the buildings along Ippokratous Avenue are all jewels of Kos town.

The castle

The most impressive and imposing building on the island is the Castle of the Knights, which stands on the north-eastern side of the harbour, ideally situated to defend Kos town and control the narrow strait between the island and the mainland of Asia Minor. It was built by the Knights of St John.

The Knights arrived on Kos towards the middle of the 14th century. They immediately realised how important it would be to fortify the town and thus protect the island. We cannot be sure that they began to build on an empty site: they may well have found the remains of the walls of a Byzantine (or even earlier) fortress, which they incorporated into their own structure. However, we know that they had no hesitation in using sections from ancient buildings, which became part of their walls.

Today, many ancient stones, pieces of marble, sections of columns and other architectural members from ancient monuments can be seen in the medieval castle. One can only guess at the severity and extent of the damage which the Knights caused to the ancient monuments of the island (destruction which the Turks continued still more systematically at a later date).

The Castle as we see it today consists of two main groups of buildings, an inner (and older) group, and an outer group. The inner enceinte, which is rectangular in shape, was begun in the time of Fantino Guerini, Venetian governor of Kos in 1436-1453. Work was continued by his successors, and completed in 1478, under the Grand Master Edoardo di Carmadino. Later it was concluded that an outer ring of defences would also be necessary to protect the inner enceinte against the developments which had occurred in the military arts in the meantime (and, in particular, against the greater firepower of the artillery). And so the building of the outer enceinte, with stronger walls, began in around 1495, under the command of Grand Master d'Aubusson.

Construction continued through the time of d'Ambois and further additions were made in 1514, under Del Carretto. The fact that the work of building the Castle went on for many decades under a number of Grand Masters explains why there are so many coats-of-arms at various places on the inner and outer walls.

Under the Turkish occupation which began in 1523 the new owners of the Castle repaired its walls and continued to use it. Indeed, for many years it was forbidden for Christians to enter the walls of the Castle.

Piri Reis, the greatest Turkish cartographer, who lived at the time when the Ottomans were preparing to capture the Greek islands, wrote of Kos that «this is a Greek island, but one which we must conquer. It is fertile, and, after Rhodes, has the best buildings. There is plenty of water, and crops abound. The placenames are Greek, such as Nerantzia, Antimacheia, Yali, Kyrio, Palamida, Kefalos, Pyli.

Kos is heavily fortified. It has four castles.» Reis then goes on to describe the castles and the harbour, drawing the attention of the aggressors to the fact that "a thousand ships could anchor" off the largest castle.

In the Middle Ages there was a moat on the city side of the castle (where Phoinikon Avenue is today), filled with sea water. In this way the castle appeared to be standing on a little island.

The main entrance faced the 'plane Tree of Hippocrates.' There were three arched bridges and a narrow passage, together with a drawbridge.

Today, we can see sections of the walls, towers, battlements and staircases, together with a series of galleries, roads, corridors and gates in the inner and outer enceintes.

The most impressive view of the Castle of the Knights on Kos is to be had by walking along the western section of the outer wall. The most imposing of the towers is that of Del Carretto, a semi-circular structure in the south-west corner of the outer enceinte.

Under the bridge which leads to the castle gate, in Phoinikon Avenue, and in many other parts of Kos town we can see remnants of the circular wall which the Knights built between 1391 and 1396 in order to protect the town from attack.

Views from the Castle.

Antiquities in the West Zone

The western part of the town has quite a number of interesting antiquities. Many of these were able to survive in relatively good condition because no-one thought to use them or demolish them in the Middle Ages. The most important antiquities in this area are as follows:

-The Hellenistic **gymnasium** with its famous xystos. The xystos was the part of the ancient gymnasium covered by a roof, where athletics could take place even in wet and wintry weather. The athletes would smear their bodies with olive oil before the games, and afterwards would wash to remove it.

A line of column along the Xystos has been restored and make an impressive sight. In the Roman era, the Hellenistic Gymnasium was modified. A pool in which the athletes could wash their hair was constructed in the centre, and the city's western baths were added. A large and imposing basilica was later erected on the site of the baths: the baptistery and a section of the sanctuary have survived.

The 'chamber of enlightenment,' or ante-chamber to the baptistery, has a fine mosaic. On the northern extremity of the Gymnasium is the floor of a house with an exceptionally fine mosaic showing the Nine Muses, Apollo Musagetes, Paris and Hermes offering the apple to Aphrodite (whom the former had judged more beautiful than Hera and Athena), and Dionysius.

To the east of the xystos restoration work has been done on a peristyle building in the Corinthian order, which in Roman times was the forica or latrine of the baths. Here, too (to the east of the xystos), a street - the Via Cardo - has come to light, with a number of houses whose floors are adorned with mosaics. Of particular interest is that showing the Rape of Europa (in the Europa House). Some statues from the same house are in the Archaeological Museum of Kos. The lavatory, too, has survived: the paintings on its walls showed the members of various professions. The picture of the postman had an inscription saying, "I spend all twelve hours of the day running." Another house in the same district had a fine mosaic showing a wild boar hunt and gladiators, together with painted scenes.

- The **Nymphaion** was built in the 3rd century BC. Some parts of its fine mosaics have survived. Eleven columns stood along three of its sides: the fourth was a wall with three recesses, in each of which was a bath. Near the Nymphaeum is a staircase leading to the Acropolis.

- The **Odeion** has survived in quite good condition. It was built in the 2nd century AD and thick walls had to be used to support its curved tiers of seating, since there was no natural amphitheatre into which it could be fitted. The lower part of the ancient structure has survived in its original form, and much of the seating has been reconstructed. Nearby a fine mosaic showing birds and fruit has been found, and many

1

statues (including one of Hippocrates) were discovered in the Odeion itself.

- The **Roman House** ('Casa Romana'). This is a large decorated house with wonderful mosaics, wall-paintings and reliefs. The building had three open courtyards. One true masterpiece is the Hellenistic mosaic made of the most delicate tesserae (which must have been shifted here from a much earlier building). It shows a tiger attacking a deer, and is in the first of the courtyards. In the second courtyard, there are mosaics around a tank (a Nereid on a sea-horse, a line of dolphins, etc.), while further along is the banqueting hall, which was decorated in a multitude of colours.

In the next room are wall-paintings showing a soldier and a number of Roman nobles (perhaps the owner and his family). In the third and largest court are two lines of Ionic columns along three sides, with Corinthian columns made of single pieces of stone on the south side. There is also a decorative balcony, a decorative pool and more mosaics (a tiger, a leopard, etc.).

- The **temple** and **altar of Dionysius**, close to the Roman House in a north-easterly direction. These are Hellenistic buildings which were also in use in the Roman period.

- The Harbour Baths or **«circular baths»**. These are on the north-west side of the harbour. They take their alternative name from the fact that the rooms in the bathhouse are arranged in a circular manner.

- The **starting-gate** of the Ancient Stadium, dating from the 2nd century BC, which is opposite the church of Ayia Anna. The dimensions of the stadium were approximately 200x14 metres. The starting-gate was the place from which the umpires gave the signal for races to begin.

1. Statue of Artemis, 2nd century BC. Kos Archaeological Museum.
2. The Hellenistic Gymnasium.

2

Antiquities in the Central Zone

In the centre of the town some traces have survived of a necropolis dating from the Early Geometric and Geometric periods, and of a Mycenean settlement.

In the eastern part of this area, in the 'house of bronze statues', bronze statuettes of Isis, Aphrodite, Ares and Demeter have been found. To the south of the church of Ayia Paraskevi are a number of Roman buildings with rooms full of mosaics and other decorative scenes. Of particular importance is a mosaic showing the arrival of Asklepios in Kos by ship: a citizen is welcoming him, while Hippocrates can be seen seated nearby. This work, dat-ing from the 3rd or 2nd century AD, is now in Kos Museum (see p. 59). The necropolis to which we have already referred contained the tombs of 77 children and infants together with a number of adult graves. Many of the valuable vessels of the Geometric and Mycenean periods which came to light in the necropolis and the adjacent Mycenean settlement can be admired in the Archaeological Museum of Kos.

Many of the wonderful mosaics found in this area were taken by the Knights to Rhodes, where they were used to decorate the Palace of the Grand Master. Among them were fine scenes showing Poseidon

1. The Nymphaion.
2. The Odeion.

fighting the giant Polybotes, Orpheus with Autumn personified, a fish, a dog hunting hares, and a personification of Constantinople.

Antiquities in the Eastern Zone

Most of the buildings of the town of the Knights, protected by the outer wall, stood in the area leading away from the Castle and bounded by Akti Miaouli, Ippokratous Avenue, Eleftherias Square and Akti Koundouriotou. Since the earthquake of 1933 which laid waste the more modern town, this area has also yielded important antiquities of various periods. The most valuable of these antiquities are as follows:

- **Sections of a Hellenistic wall** which surrounded the town in the 4th century BC. This can be seen at various points in the modern town. in some places, its thickness is as much as 6 or 8 metres. The wall starts on the eastern edge of the town of the Knights, by a Hellenistic sanctuary. One branch then turns west, passes next to the Agora and crosses the site of the Museum. Another branch sets out from the Hellenistic sanctuary and runs down to the harbour, where the impressive Palace of the Regent stands, like a medieval castle. A fourth section can be seen at the harbour baths, from which it goes as far as the sea.

- The 4th- or 3rd-century BC **Stoa**, with its impressive restored columns. Here was found the fine head of Marsyas, now to be seen in the Archaeological Museum of Kos.

- The great basilica in the Orthodox cemetery of the town. From the magnificence of its baptistery one can imagine the grandeur of the church as a whole. It stood on the site formerly occupied by the Stoa mentioned above. Historians calculate that the basilica was built in the 5th or 6th century, and that it measured 73 x 23.5 metres. The baptistery was later renamed St John of the Seven Steps, and was dedicated to St John the Baptist. The popular name 'the seven steps' came from the four apses in its corners, the apse of the sanctuary and the two recesses in the north and south walls.

- The **ancient Agora,** or forum, on Ippokratous Avenue, which covered a total area of 160x80 square metres. Two of its columns have been restored, and now resemble a kind of entrance archway. The church of St Constantine was built on the site of the Agora: it dates from around the same period as the great basilica in the Orthodox cemetery and has some traces of wall-paintings.

Nearby, apart from St Constantine, are the interesting churches of Ayios Ioannis the Martyr (burned alive by the Turks), the Panayia (Virgin Mary) Gorgoepikos, the Panayia Katevati and Ayios Georgios.

-The **Hellenistic sanctuary**, which we have already mentioned in our description of the walls. This was probably built in the 2nd century BC, and is trapezoidal in shape. To the south of the Hellenistic sanctuary some outstanding mosaic floors have come to light, showing a fisherman, Orpheus with animals and the symposium of Herakles.

- The **Sanctuary of Herakles,** which measured 12 metres by 9. Part of a statue of Herakles which was probably inside the sanctuary and showing his lion-skin, is built into the south corner of the Loggia Mosque.

-The **Sanctuary of Aphrodite Pandemos,** with drums from Corinthian columns. Near the sanctuary is a fine mosaic dating from the Early Christian period and showing animal heads. The town of Kos is famed for its large number of historical monuments. In order to assist the visitor in the best tour of the archaeological sites, we have divided the town into west, east and central archaeological zones.

The ancient Agora and antiquities from the east zone.

The Museum

The building was erected by the Italians. Its imposing facade, an imitation of the city's Roman baths, contains three entrances, with steps. The Museum building consists of an antechamber, three galleries on the ground floor (east, north and west) and an upper floor. The exhibits to be seen are as follows:

- An impressive mosaic dating from the 2nd or 3rd century AD, showing the arrival on the island of Asklepios. He is being received by a Koan, while Hippocrates is watching the ceremony from in front of a rock near a cave.

This mosaic, in the peristyle of the Museum, was found in 1935 during excavations to the south of the church of Ayia Paraskevi. For a while it was moved to Rhodes, but it eventually came back to Kos.

- Cylindrical and rectangular funerary altars, most of them dating from the Hellenistic period. Among the decorative motifs used are the heads of oxen, garlands, flowers, the cornucopeia.
- A head of Alexander the Great (3rd century BC).
- Sections of funerary stelai of the 6th and 5th centuries BC.
- A huge head of the goddess Demeter.
- A Roman frieze showing a horse's head.
- A frieze with a lion figure, which was once built into the wall of the Castle of the Knights.

1. Statue of Hermes. It was found in the House of Europa. 2nd century BC.
2. Statue of a woman that was found in the Odeion.

1

2

- A head of Trajan.
- A marble table of the Roman period with lion's paws.
- The funerary frieze of a dead man elevated to heroic stature, on a ship (2nd century BC).
- A statue of the goddess Artemis with a quiver and arrows and a little dog by her side (2nd century AD).
- A statue of the goddess Hygeia carrying a snake and holding out an egg, with a symbolic depiction of love or sleep (2nd century AD).
- Headless female statues with traces of paint (2nd century AD).

A headless statue of the god Asklepios with a snake on one side and the demon Telesphorus on the other (2nd century AD).
- Relief supports for tables depicting the heads of the gods Dionysius and Grypas (2nd century AD).
- A head (perhaps of Perseus) dating from the Hellenistic period.
-A head of Antoninus Pius.
- Heads of statues from the Roman period (men, youth, girl, woman).
- A Roman statue of the god Hermes seated on a rock; he has a winged hat, winged sandals and a magic wand or sceptre (see p. 29).
- Two torsos of Ephesian Artemis (recognisable by the number of breasts).

3. Headless statue of Asklepios, 2nd century BC.
4. Group sculpture with the god Dionysus, Pan and a Satyr. The god Eros is at their feet. 2nd century BC.

3

4

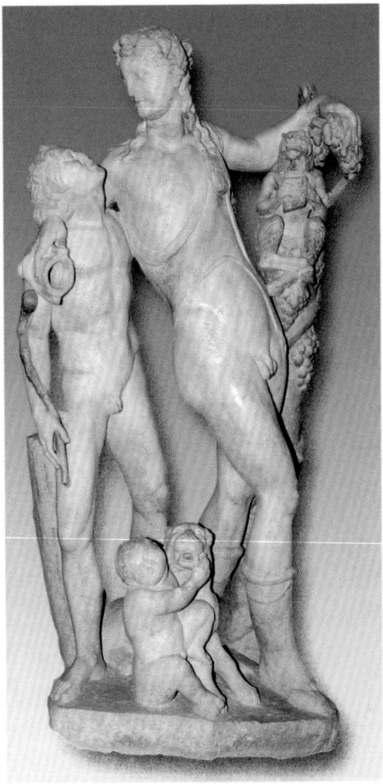

1

- A headless Roman statue of the goddess Demeter.
- Torsos of Roman statues of the goddess Hygeia, clothed women, etc.
- A Roman table support showing Marsyas hanged.
- A group of Aphrodite and a small cupid (1 st century AD).
-A statue of the Muse Clio (Hellenistic period).
- A relief showing a banquet scene (6th century BC).
- A Hellenistic statue of Aphrodite bearing arms.
- A section of a relief dating from the 6th century BC, showing a boy holding a cockerel.

2

3

- Votive offerings to Hades (3rd century BC).
- Statues of the goddesses Demeter and Persephone (her daughter), dating from the 4th century BC.
- A statuette of a young satyr.
- A statue of a cupid (copy of a work by the famous sculptor Praxiteles).

1. Head of a wounded warrior, Hellenistic period.
2. Tomb stele.
3. Mosaic of the 2nd or 3rd century, depicting Asklepios' arrival on the island.
4. Statue of a woman that was found in the Odeion.
5. Statue of the Goddess Tyche, 1st century BC.

4

5

ITINE

A few years ago, touring Kos was no easy business. Today, however, it is a simple undertaking. Starting at Kos town, there are two basic routes, one towards Psalidi and Ayios Fokas, and the other to Kefalos and Ayios Ioannis. It is easy to drive around the whole island in a single day, given that the longest distance by road is 49 kilometres. This is the route from the main town to Kefalos and Ayios Ioannis, in the most south-westerly part of the island. We reach this point after crossing the narrowest part of Kos.
The scenery changes constantly and rapidly, now consisting of mountains, now of the sea, now of fields, now of cosmopolitan beaches and now of quaint little villages. However, accommodation in the form of hotels and rented rooms is to be found everywhere, as are restaurants.

More specifically, our routes on the island are as follows:

1. Psalidi - Ayios Fokas -Thermes
2. Platani - Asklepeion
3. Zipari - Asfendiou - Tingaki
4. Linopotis -Marmari - Pyli
5. Antimacheia -Kardamaina - Mastihari
6. Paradeisos - Ayios Stefanos - Kefalos Ayios Ioannis

Make sure to visit...

Beaches:
- Ayios Fokas, p. 76, 77
- Lambi, p. 76
- Psalidi, p. 76, 77
- Thermes, p. 77
- Tingaki, p. 80, 92
- Marmari, p. 80, 94
- Kardamaina, p. 96-99
- Mastihari, p. 96, 99, 101
- Paradeisos, p.102
- Ayios Stefanos, p. 102

Churches Monasteries:
- Ayios Gavriel, p. 77
- Ayios Pavlos, p. 90
- Evangelistria, p. 90, 91

Archaeological Sites:
- Roman tombs, p. 80
- Asklepion, p. 80 - 82, 85 - 87
- Ayios Theodoros, p. 94
- Ayia Paraskevi, p. 105
- Ancient Halassarni, p. 98
- Ayios Ioannis, p. 66, 74, 102, 103, 107
- Kefalos, p. 80, 102, 103, 105

Castles:
- Pyli, p. 102
- Antimacheia, p. 94, 96-102
- Kardamaina, p. 95-99

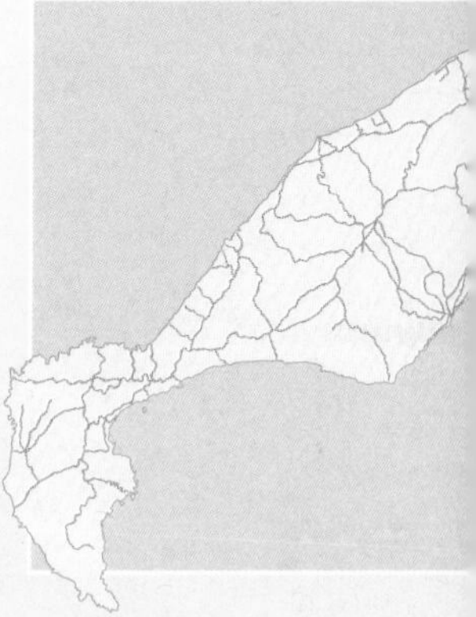

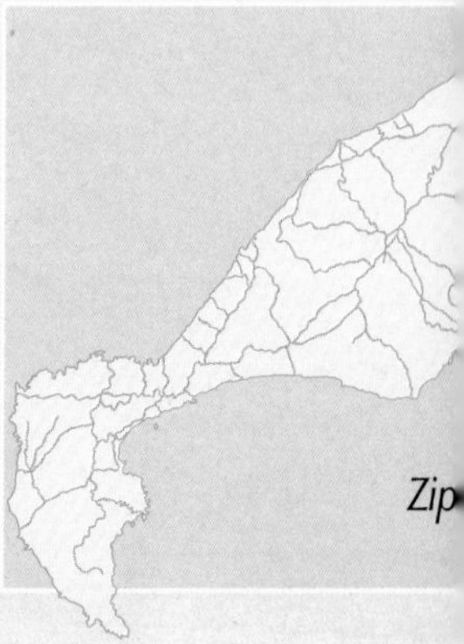

RIES ON THE ISLAND

ROUTE 1
kas -Thermes
pages 76-79

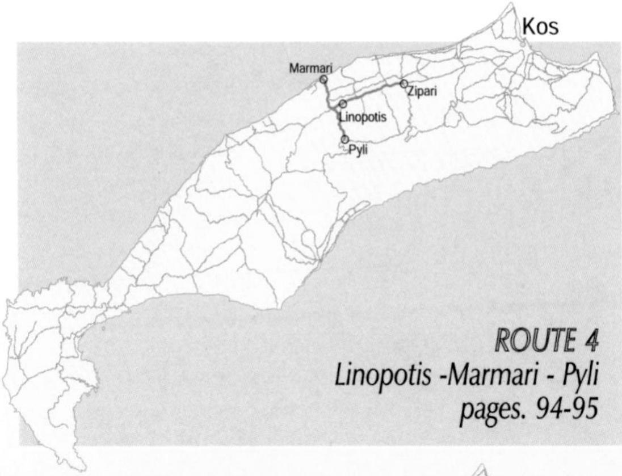

ROUTE 4
Linopotis -Marmari - Pyli
pages. 94-95

ROUTE 2
- Asklepeion
pages 80-89

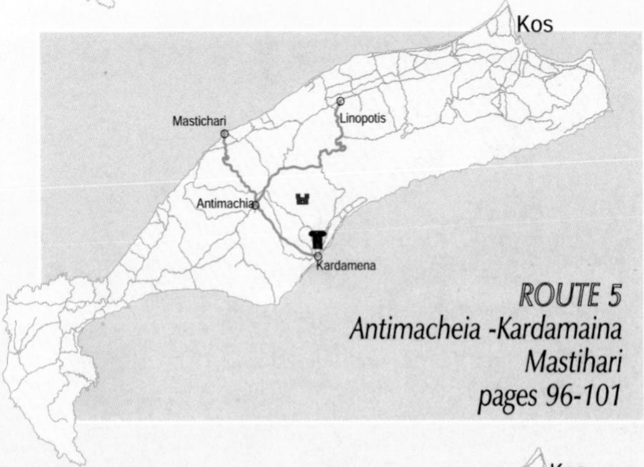

ROUTE 5
Antimacheia -Kardamaina
Mastihari
pages 96-101

ROUTE 3
ou - Tingaki
pages 90-93

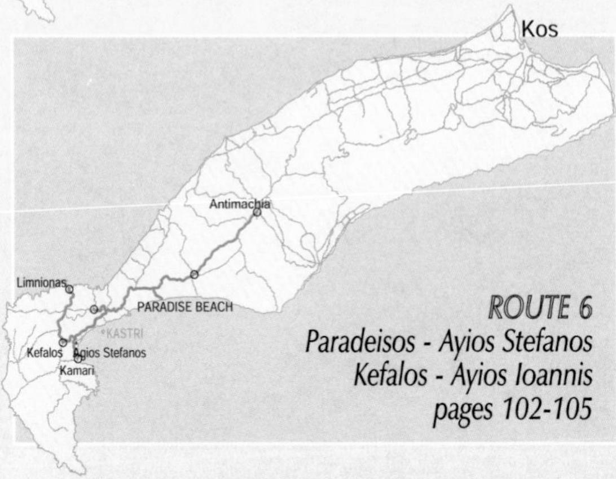

ROUTE 6
Paradeisos - Ayios Stefanos
Kefalos - Ayios Ioannis
pages 102-105

ROUTE 1
Psalidi - Ayios Fokas Thermes

Our firsth route crosses the eastern coast. We will then have the chance to visit the capes Psalidi and Ayios Fokas. Finally, our tour ends at Thermes

1

Take Phoinikon Avenue leading out of Kos town, heading in an easterly direction. In earlier days, the area around the bridge, with its bougainvillias, was a popular spot with cyclists, who could be seen spinning along on early evening rides on the seafront. Even today, bicycles are just as attractive a mode of transport.

After 2 km you will arrive at Paradeisi, an area where there are numerous hotels, and after 3km to the Psalidi area, with hotels and a camp site.

Further down Kanaris Street (4 km. from Kos town) you will reach **Lambi** with its white, sandy beaches. Bars, cafes, water sports and loud music are some of the things you will find at Lambi.

Cape **Psalidi**, or **Louros**, resembles the blade of a pair of scissors -

2

hence its name - and is 4.5 km from Kos town. The seasonal Pseftopotamos river has its estuary just beyond Psalidi.

Continuing along the same road, you will arrive after 8 km at the excellent beach of **Ayios Fokas**, which has brilliantly clear water and large hotel com-plexes. In 1974, excavations in the area of the Dimitra Hotel brought to light a farmhouse of the Roman period. To the east of **Ayios Gavriel**, the remains of an Early Christian basilica have been found.

Cape Ayios Fokas is a steeply-sloping arm protruding from a hill with a height of some 75 metres above sea-level, in which the island's mountain chain comes to an end. In the post-Byzantine period there was a little chapel dedicated to Ayios Fokas in the vicinity.

1. The new marina outside Kos town, heading towards Psalidi.
2. The beach at Lambi.
3. The Early Christian basilica of Ayios Gavriel.

Thermes, a well-organised resort village with a **medicinal spring**, is 13 km from Kos town. The spring water is used for hydrotherapy for the treatment of rheumatism, arthritis and gynaecological complaints.

The drinking water of the area is refreshing and good for the digestion.

Some kilometres to the south-west is the warm bubbling spring known as 'sta piso Thermi.'

A small monastery to Ayia Irene can also be seen

3

here, underground: the buildings, of which traces can be identified, are very old.

Minor tracks and footpaths lead on from this point.

Psalidi (above) and Thermes (below and right)

ROUTE 2
Platani - Asklepeion

The second route starts in Kos town and takes you to Platani before ending at the Asklepeion.

This route is of the greatest archaeological interest on Kos, since it includes a tour of the Asklepeion and the International Hippocrates Foundation. The Asklepeion is today believed to be the earliest hospital which the ancient world can boast of. It had wards, surgeries and visiting rooms, all of which came to light during the course of excavations.

The Asklepion.

The main road leads out of Kos town in a south-westerly direction. Approximately 2 km from the town you will come to the village of **Platani**, known in Turkish times as Kermetes as a result of the fact that convicts from Keramos in Asia Minor were brought here and settled around an open prison in the village. The name Platani comes from the plane tree ('platanos') which used to grow in the main square. In effect, Platani is now part of the town of Kos. Yet there are still unusual features about its houses and its inhabitants.

Most of the houses are old, and there are traditional coffee-shops where coffee of the most authentic kind is served.

Platani has both an Orthodox church and a Muslim mosque.

To the west of the village square are the ruins of a magnificent Roman tomb. Another such structure can be seen shortly before we enter Platani. In the Christian era it was converted and used as a church.

The Archaeological Museum of Istanbul contains an inscription that was found at Platani by the antiquarian Ioannis Kallisperis of Kalymnos. The

1

inscription gives detailed information about the ancient Greek tax system. It dates from the 2nd century BC, when Rhodes was in alliance with Kos and the surrounding islands, and it functioned as a regulation of the Koan state.

The Asklepeion

About 3 km from the town, a turning to our left (south-east) allows us to visit the famous Asklepeion of Kos (about 1 km from the turning on the main road). The site of the sanctuary is very beautiful, and there is a wonderful view across Kos town and the coast of Asia Minor beyond. The ancient Koans made creative use of the folds in the terrain of a little hill to erect the various buildings on three different levels.

Our information about the founding of the first sanctuaries of Asklepios fades out in the mists of pre-history. Asklepios himself is a mysterious figure: according to the ancient Greek myths, he was the god of health and medicine, son of Apollo; in another version, he was a mortal who lived in the 13th century BC and was deified at some later date.

We know of some 300 sanctuaries to him right across the ancient world, of which the most famous were those at Trikke in Thessaly (where Asklepios is reputed to have been born), Epidaurus, Kos, Athens and Leros (where the water from the Paliaskloupi spring, which once served the Asklepeion, is still drunk today). The Asklepeion of Kos became particularly famous in ancient times thanks to the skill and wisdom of its Asklepiads (doctors) and in particular of the most eminent of them all, Hippocrates, the father of medicine, who founded the world's first school of medicine on the island.

The buildings of the Asklepeion were first excavated by the German archaeologist Rudolf Herzog in 1902, after his attention had repeatedly been drawn to the site by the local author and antiquarian Iakovos E. Zaraftis.

1, 2. Views from Platani.

2

Strabo describes its buildings with great admiration, and has much to say of the valuable votive offerings and important works of art they contained. He tells us that it was 'a most glorious sanctuary full of votive offerings, including the Antigonus of Apelles and Aphrodite Rising from the Sea' (the latter was a famous statue by the great sculptor Praxiteles, specially commissioned by the city of Kos).

The International Hippocratic Foundation of Kos is based near the Asklepeion. It stands in an estate of 24 hectares just above the village of Platani, and its aims are the promotion of scientific research by doctors of all nationalities, the awarding of prizes to medical authors and for medical discoveries, and the publication of the works of Hippocrates and of manuscripts on Hippocratic medicine. There are plans to build a modern 'city of Hippocrates' in the vicinity: each five years, representatives of the world's doctors will gather here for an international medical Olympiad. Around the Asklepeion was a sacred grove, in which - according to Pausanias - it was forbidden for anyone to be born or die.

According to the accounts of ancient travellers, the Asklepeion contained a large open space shaded by plane trees. Between the first and second terraces a series of fountains had been constructed, and sulphurous and ferruginous water gushed out. This was the hydrotherapy area. These fountains were served by clay pipes which brought water to the Asklepeion from the Vourina spring or spring of Hippocrates. Now the spring is known as 'Kokkino nero' (red water). Apart from its iron content, the water also contains significant quantities of calcium and magnesium salts as well as free carbonic acid.

The Vourina spring or spring of King Chalkon lies approximately one hour from Kos town in the foothills of Mt Dikaios, at the far end of a dark tunnel. For some three thousand years, crystal-clear water has flowed from the spring to provide the water supply of Kos town. The spring was praised by Theocritus in his Idylls. There is a vaulted building with polygonal masonry, probably of the Hellenistic period, a hole in the top of which provides light and ventilation. The spring itself is inside a conical chamber with a perimeter of 10 metres and a height of 7 metres. A dark tunnel 30 metres in length leads into the chamber. Inside the chamber is an aperture from which the water to supply the town wells out. This concealed rock is rather like the snout of an ox, and it may be from this resemblance (voos-rinos = ox's snout) that the name 'Vourina' is derived. Above the tunnel is a little room which was probably used to guard the tunnel.

The ancient traditions say that the mythical King Chalkon of Kos kicked the rock and the spring burst forth into what Theocritus describes as a cool grove of leafy trees - poplars and elms. From there it was led down to the plane-tree of Hippocrates before entering the town supply.

LEGEND

FIRST TERRACE
1. Access staircase (24 steps)
2. Propylaia
3. Statue bases
4. Roman buildings
5. Colonnadeά
6. Patients' rooms
7. Retaining wall with recesses
8. Staircase to second terrace (30 steps)

SECOND TERRACE
9. Temple of Asklepios
10. Altar of Asklepios
11. Temple of Apollo
12. Club
13. Exedra
14. Priests' quarters
15. Staircase to third terrace (60 steps)

THIRD TERRACE
16. Great Temple of Asklepios
17. Stoas
18. Patients' rooms

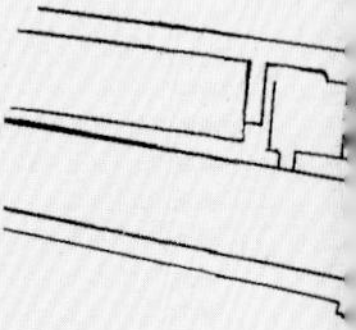

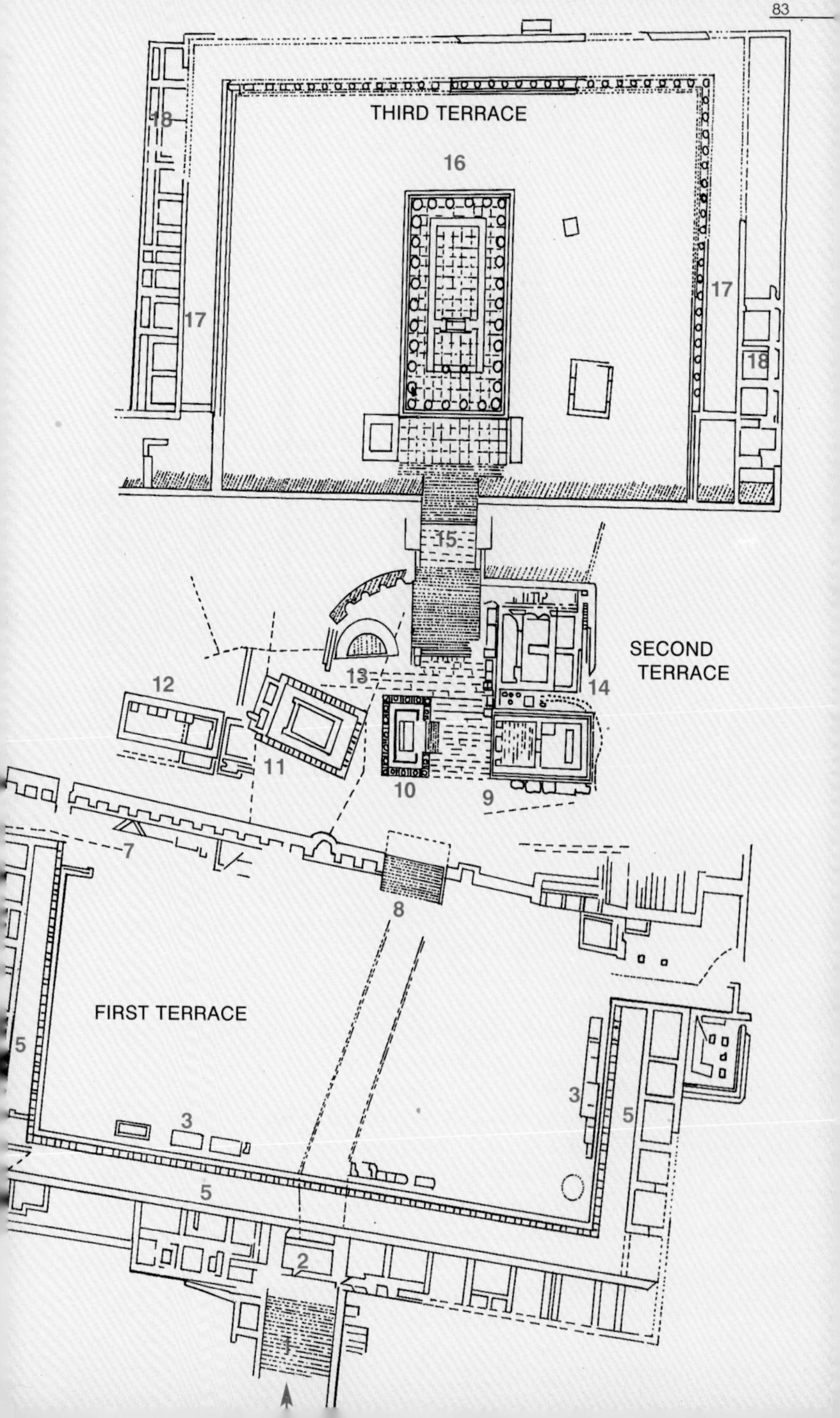
THIRD TERRACE
16
18
17
17
18
15
SECOND TERRACE
12
13
14
11
10
9
7
8
FIRST TERRACE
5
3
3
5
5
2
1

Climbing the Terraces

The **first terrace** of the Asklepeion is reached by a staircase with 24 steps from the propylaia. On three sides of this terrace was a colonnade behind which were rooms (their foundations can be seen). Historians have posited that this may have been the famous school of medicine, which also possessed an anatomical and pathological museum.

It was in at least some of these rooms that patients and their families stayed for their first examination by the physicians. On the south side of the terrace, facing the opening in the colonnade, is a retaining wall to hold up the earth above and behind it. The restored niches in it were occupied by statues. The colonnade appears to date from the 3rd century BC. Two underground rooms found inside the outer wall contained large numbers of votive statuettes depicting the sick or their diseased members and portraying the attitudes of the body characteristic of the disease. It has been hypothesised by some that there was a temple to Aphrodite on the same spot, holding the famous statue by Praxiteles.

We climb to the **second terrace** on a staircase with 30 steps. To the left,

The columns of the temple of Apollo.

in a recess, is a depiction of the god Pan with his pipes, from beneath the feet of which water flows. To the right of the staircase an inscription has survived from the small temple of the famous Koan physician Gaius Stertinius Xenophon, who held priestly rank at the Asklepeion and was the personal doctor of the Emperor Claudius.

Nearby, to the west, are the remains of baths which may have been used for hydrotherapy.

In the middle of the second terrace are the remains of the oldest structure on the site, an altar to Apollo Cyparissus. The second terrace also contained buildings dedicated to Asklepios and all the other deities associated with health and medicine more generally.

A temple containing an altar to Asklepios (with two restored columns) is dated by some scholars to the 4th century BC and by others to the 3rd. This altar was reached up a slope from the west, thus making it easier for the sacrificial animals to approach. Around it was a small colonnade, and next to this were the famous statues of Asklepios, Hygeia and Apione, works of Cephissodotus and Timachus, the sons of Prax-iteles. In the cella of the temple was a rectangular opening lined with granite slabs: this was used as a treasury, and visitors and patients would drop their offerings and gifts into it.

The temple is in the Ionian order. Nearby are the ruins of buildings dating from the Roman period. These were the priests' houses. Close at hand was the abaton, to which entry was not permitted, where the sacred spring rose. A short distance from the altar is a semi-circular raised platform, presumably for outdoor meetings of the priests. To the east of the altar of Asklepios traces have come to light of a peripteral temple of Apollo in the Corinthian order (of which two sides have been restored). Still further to the east is a ruined building of the Hellenistic period. On the very edge of the terrace, to the west, was a small temple dedicated to Nero. Traces have been found of a staircase linking the various buildings with the sacred grove. The staircase to the third terrace has 60 steps, with a break in the middle. Here, too, there are retaining walls.

The **third terrace** measures 80 metres by 100. Scanty traces of a colonnade around three of its sides have come to light, as well as of

The Asklepeion.

buildings of the Hellenistic period. In the middle of the terrace, facing the point where the staircase emerges, is the large ruined temple of Asklepios, built in the Doric order in the 2nd century BC.

There were also huge statues of Asklepios and Hygeia on the third terrace. The temple of Asklepios had dimensions of 34x18 metres, and 108 columns. On the east side is a large marble plaque and a column capital on which the letters IXCP (one of the better-known acronyms for the name of Christ) have been carved.

This was the altar of a Christian church which has now disappeared. Behind the colonnade mentioned above are traces of rooms, most likely used as accommodation for the sick. Also on the third and last terrace - which stands 100 metres above sea level - are traces of a 5th century temple, possibly to Apollo.

At the southernmost extremity of the colonnade was a staircase linking the terrace to the sacred grove. From high up on the third terrace we have a superb view over the flat part of the island and across towards the coast of Asia Minor in the Halicarnassus area.

FONDATION INTERNATIONALE HIPPOCRATIQUE DE COS

ΔΙΕΘΝΕΣ ΙΠΠΟΚΡΑΤΕΙΟΝ ΙΔΡΥΜΑ ΤΗΣ ΚΩ

1960

The International Hippocratic Foundation

The International Hippocratic Foundation of Kos is based near the Asklepeion. It stands in an estate of 24 hectares just above the village of Platani, and its aims are the promotion of scientific research by doctors of all nationalities, the awarding of prizes to medical authors and for medical discoveries, and the publication of the works of Hippocrates and of manuscripts on Hippocratic medicine.

Route 3
Zipari - Asfendiou

(Evangelistria - Asomatos - Lagoudi - Zia - Ayios Dimitrios) ***- Tingaki***

Our third route starts in Kos town as usual and runs along the main road as far as Zipari. We then head south for Asfendiou, with its numerous different settlements and rich folklore tradition. Shortly after Zipari a turning to the right takes us to Tingaki, on the coast.

We leave the town in a westerly direction. We pass the turning for the Asklepeion and carry straight on. After 9 km we enter the lowland village of **Zipari**, which came into being as a settlement of people from Asfendiou.

The ruins of Early Christian churches have been found in the vicinity. One of the many Early Christian (5th-6th century) churches to have come to light in Kos was found at Zipari during excavations in 1935. This was the basilica of Ayios Pavlos, measuring 21.60 x 15 metres. It stood at the northern end of a village which may have been the ancient deme of Phyxiotes.

According to the archaeologist Orlandos, this was a large complex of ecclesiastical buildings concentrated around the basilica, with houses for the priests and other areas of worship. In the church itself, the foundations of the pulpit can be distinguished, with two steps up to it, and in the south-west corner the walls stand to a considerable height.

There is a baptistery there, with a cruciform font in its centre.

In 1935, another basilica was discovered to the south of the basilica of Ayios Pavlos. Known as the Kapamas basilica from its site, this church measures 17 x 16.30 metres. Its baptistery is of the greatest interest: it is circular, with a dome, and there are recesses in the walls for doors and domed passages. The font is cruciform, and there are unusual mosaics.

To the east of Zipari, at Platanaki, is the underground chapel of Ayios Ioannis Hostos (Hidden). Dedicatory letters to the Monastery of Patmos indicate that the chapel was built in the 16th century. The altar and traces of icons remain. A section of the road continues further south from Zipari and ascends the slope of Mt Dikaios. After about five kilometres it reaches the largest and most pretty of all the island's villages, with the largest number of quarters: Afendiou.

Asfendiou is built on the mountain's highest peak, and is a wonderful place to stay, both in the summer and winter. The region is a luscious green, with plenty of running water. Local produce includes grapes, olives, tomatoes, garden vegetables, etc. The view from the heights here to the coasts of Asia Minor is magical.

The quarters of Asfendiou are: Evangelistria, Asomatos, Lagoudi (at a height of 240 m.), Zia (above 350 m.) and Ayios Dimitrios (Haihoutes), which is no longer inhabited. In the houses of these quarters one will come across completely white gardens full of flowers.

The first quarter which we encounter is **Evangelistria** with the large church of the Evangelismos in the square. The next quarter of **Asomatos** contains a fine 18th-century church of the Archangels, which celebrates its feast day on 8 November. On this day there a great festival takes place with a Pan-Koan pilgrimage.

Views from Asfendiou.

Zia is on the slopes of Mt Dikaios, and is verdant with many springs. Zia has been designated a settlement of especial beauty and a protected area, as has the whole of Asfendiou.

At **Zia**, at the foothills of the mountain, the little church which belonged to a small monastery has been preserved, known as the **Monastery of the Spondes**. It is dedicated to the Panayia and tradition holds that it was founded in the 11th century by the Blessed Christodoulos. At the most southern point of Zia, at the foot of the mountain in nearby Kefalovrysi, there is a small dependency of the monastery with a chapel of the Eisodion of the Theotokos, beneath the sanctuary of which there gushes plenty of water. The festival which takes place here on 21 November gathers many pilgrims from all over the island. At the peak of Mt Dikaios there is another little church that belonged to a small monastery, known as the Monastery of Sotiros (Saviour) Christos, or the Monastery of the Dikaios (Just) Christos. It was built by the Koan monk Arsenios Skinouris in 1079 and for many years, according also to a Byzantine imperial Chrysobul, it collected financial support for the monks.

It was built in the days of the Blessed Christodoulos, when the Byzantine Emperor gave part of Kos to the Christodoulos in order to collect money so that he could build the monastery of Patmos. From this point the whole of the island and the surrounding sea can be seen, as can, further off, the islands of Tilos,

1

Nisyros, Kalymnos, Pserimos, Leros, Patmos, Samos and Astypalaia, along with the opposite Asia Minor coast and Cnidus.

In the vicinity of Asfendiou one can also visit the old churches of the Panayia Monagriou, Panayia Tsakali, Stavros and Ayia Marina. There are also, albeit not exploited today, lead, silver and marble mines.

From Asfendiou we can reach Pyli by following the road in a westerly direction for 4 kilometres.

2

In the vicinity of Asfendiou we will encounter not only Zipari, but also the coastal resort of **Tingaki**. A section of the road leads out from Zipari in a north-westerly direction to reach Tingaki. This is a delightful resort (it is around 3 km. from Zipari and 6,5 from Afendiou), which in the summer months is filled with Greek and foreign tourists.

Traces of an old church of Ayios Georgios canbe seen at the site of Voukolia in Tingaki.

3

Tingaki has hotels and furnished rooms which spread out over a verdant region. This is a great tourist resort, with many tourist offices, shops, cafes, bars, facilities for water sports, and an organised beach.

1. The Panayia Kyparotissa. 2. The Moñastery of Spondes.
3. Evangelistria. Below and opposite page: Tingaki.

4

ROUTE 4
Linopotis -Marmari - Pyli

From Zipari we take the main road across the island as far as Linopotis.
From Linopotiss, side-roads to the right and left lead down to the cosmopolitan seaside resort of Marmari and the farming centre of Pyli inland.

From Zipari, the main road continues in a south-westerly direction. After about 4 km we come to a crossroads. This is Linopotiss, 13 km from Kos town.

Linopotiss was built by Italian settlers, whom the Italian government installed in the area after 1925, giving them large areas of land which had formerly belonged to local Greeks. In the vicinity is a large spring known as 'Limni' ('the lake'), which is used to irrigate the nearby fields. The spring is described as a place of great beauty in the Idylls of Theocritus.

In 1936, archaeologists came across the remains of an ancient farm at Fouskoma, near Linopotis.

At Ayios Theodoros, on the road to **Antimacheia**, the ruins of an Early Christian basilica and the remains of a Roman aqueduct have come to light.

On the way to Pyli is a little chapel to the martyr St Claudia, known locally as Ayiaklafti.

The road which now heads to th right (north-west) ends at the attractive seaside village of **Marmari**, a popular resort for Greek and foreign visitors. It has large hotels and rented rooms, tavernas and cafes, all of which make it an ideal spot for holidays. The excellent beach is 2 km long. The other road at the crossroads soon brings us to the village of Pyli, some 15.5 kms from Kos town, at an altitude of 300 metres on the slopes of Mt Dikaios.

Above: the church of Ayios Georgios at Pyli.
Below: Marmari.

The original village of Pyli was abandoned by its inhabitants in 1830 after an epidemic of cholera and a new site chosen. The name probably

comes from the ancient word Pele, as in the ancient deme of Peletes.

This is the area where most of the island's tomatoes are produced, and the village stands in the middle of a fertile area where onions, sesame seeds and olives are also grown.

Pyli is the general name for the settlements of Ayios Georgios, Ayios Nikolaos, Konario, Peripatos and Amaniou, and it has a total population of some 2,000. At Palio Pyli, higher up, are the remains of a Byzantine castle and of an interesting 'Monastery of Our Lady', built in the 11th century by the Blessed Christodoulos. It has a marble altar resting on four columns, and parts of its wall-paintings (dating from the 14th century) have survived. The Monastery of Our Lady has its feast day on 2 February.

There are also wall-paintings in the churches of Ayios Antonios and All Saints, while in the vicinity are churches to the Prophet Elias and St Patrick.

Ayios Nikolaos at Pyli has two pleasant countryside spots, Pygi and Harmyli. The former took its name ('fountain') from a six-spouted fountain with an abundant supply of excellent water which is used to irrigate the fields and supply the local houses. The structure containing the fountain was renovated in 1592, as we can see from its inscription.

At Harmyli are some remains of the underground family tomb of the ancient Koan hero Harmylus, with hewn recesses for the dead on each side. An Early Christian church of St Basil has come to light nearby, at Konario.

On the west side of the modern village, near the spot known as Pygi, are some remains of buildings erected by the Knights (country houses and store-rooms). The general area is known as Voukolies.

According to ancient writers, the Pyli district was the site of the towns of Aleis and Pele, which had temples to Zeus and Demeter. The local people were known for their celebration of the thalysia, a harvest festival. From Pyli we can travel on to Kardamaina, 25 km from Kos town.

The Byzantine castle at Palio Pyli (above) and the village.

ROUTE 5
Antimacheia - Kardamaina - Mastihari

Route 5 begins at Linopotiss (13 km from Kos) and takes us along the main road as far as Antimacheia. From Antimacheia, a turning to the left will take us to the picturesque seaside village of Kardamaina, while a turning to the right leads to Mastihari on the north coast.

We start from Linopotiss, leaving behind the turning for Pyli and heading along the main road for Antimacheia.

At 25 km from Kos town we come to Antimacheia, one of the few places on the island to have kept its ancient name. This was the site of the ancient deme of Antimachides. Nearby (1 km from the village) is the island's international airport.

Antimacheia has a population of about 1,500, who live in the

1

various quarters into which the village is divided: Ayia Triada, Panayia (Proskynima) and Ayii Apostoli. The area produces cereals, fruit and vegetables, sesame seeds and tobacco. Livestock breeding takes place in the surrounding district. Antimacheia also has a number of picturesque windmills.

In his book Folklore of Kos, Iraklis M. Karanastasis has this to say of Antimacheia:

«In the centre of the island, at a distance of approximately one hour from each other, are the villages of Antimacheia and Kardamaina. At one time, the two villages formed a single municipality. But as our grandfathers relate, the War of Independence of 1821 found the villagers sheltering in Antimacheia castle, a large Venetian fortress that dominates the island's central plain. They had taken refuge there to escape from the cruel raids of the Algerian and Saracen corsairs who were the scourge of the Aegean in the days of piracy.

Around 1850 they moved out of the confined quarters of the castle and settled in the open land around it.

They split into two groups: one set up house on a broad and open plateau at an altitude of some 200 metres, while the other moved down

2

to the south-west of the castle and settled in a fertile valley with vines, olives and other fruit trees which is crossed by a dry river bed and lies about 20 minutes from the coast. Today, that spot is known as Old Kardamaina. They were unable to live for more than about fifty years in this pretty valley, because it became muddy whenever it rained and the malaria which raged stopped the village from developing. The local people thought the place was

1. The Castle of Antimacheia with Kardamaina in the background.
2. The Church of Ayia Paraskevi.

haunted, and for that reason the number of families was always kept at thirty-nine. As soon as a fortieth family came along, one had to move out. So towards the end of the 19th century or at the beginning of the 20th they moved away and settled on the stretch of the coast at the mouth of the valley, to the south, where the modern village of Kardamaina stands. Many of the families in one village are related to the other, bearing the same name; they are branches of the original family which lived in the castle a hundred and fifty years ago.»

There are many old churches in the area of Antimacheia: the church known as 'the Olive Grove', Ayios Georgios Dromikos, Ayia Marina and Ayios Georgios Makris.

From Antimacheia, a road runs south-east to **Kardamaina** (approximately 6 km).

The famous Venetian castle stands 3 km along this road, on the site of an earlier building. The remains of gates, rooms, stores, water tanks and other structures have survived. Inside the castle is a church of Ayia Paraskevi, where there is a popular religious and secular feast on 26 July.

This church of Ayia Paraskevi is a single-aisled basilica with a tiled roof. The floor is laid with small square tiles, and the altar consists of an Early Christian column capital. Only traces have survived of the wall-paintings. Inside the castle there are also remains of a church of Ayios Nikolaos, above the door to which is a plaque bearing the coat-of-arms of the Knights and the date 1520. There is a cistern in the precinct of the church.

After visiting the castle of Antimacheia, we continue along the main road, which leads us for another 3 km across the fertile plain to Kardamaina.

Kardamaina, half-way along the south coast of the island, is a very popular and well-loved tourist resort with fine clean beaches. The beach here has a length of 6 km.

On a hill to the north of Kardamaina stand the ruins of a castle which was built by the Knights of St John. It bears an inscription over the gate stating that construction work was finished in 1494.

The important ancient city of Halassarne or Halassarna, which was larger than the modern village, stood in the area to the south of Kardamaina. The foundations of ancient buildings, a Hellenistic theatre and other structures have been found, including an Early Christian basilica of the Godhead, which was one of the largest on the island.

At Ayia Theotis, on the boundary of the ancient deme of Malassarnites, the foundations have been found of a temple to Apollo which is the oldest on the island and was second in wealth only to the Asklepeion. The ruins of an ancient theatre and three Early Christian churches were also found in the vicinity.

In 1928, archaeologists came across the little Roman theatre of Kardamaina.

Kardamaina once had an important tradition in making pottery, and turned out large quantities of utensils of various kinds. Of its numerous potteries, only one has remained and it is now subject to a preservation order imposed by the Archaeological Service.

Kardamaina is now really an enormous hotel, capable of providing hospitality for more than 10,000 people a day. Almost all the 1,400 inhabitants are involved in tourism in one way or another. However, the Port Authority on the quay, the Lambadis house in the square and the Andriotakis olive groves on the slopes of the nearby hills are partial reminders of what Kardamaina was once like.

From Kardamaina we return to Antimacheia.

From Antimacheia, the road brings us in 5 km to Mastihari (at total of 17 km from the Linopotiss crossroads). By the side of the road is the chapel of Ayios Georgios Loizou, the walls of which contain pieces of ancient masonry. Inscriptions and other finds from the surrounding area testify to the existence here of a city called Hippia, which had a famous temple to Hera.

To the north-west of this city, near the church of Ayios Georgios, an inscription to the god Pan has been found. Another inscription refers to

Views from today's Kardamainc

the 'feast of the cutting of the trees of Hera', which the local people held every two years. Here, too, was produced the famous wine of Hippia.

The road ends at the attractive seaside village of **Mastihari**, where some of the inhabitants of Antimacheia settled after the violent earthquake of 1933.

There are superb beaches here and in the summer the hotels and rented rooms are full of holiday-makers.

The remains of an Early Christian basilica of the 5th century, with outstanding mosaics, have survived. The three-aisled basilica at Mastihari is based on eastern models. It has no atreum. The baptistery is of particular interest: it contains two sections, an ante-chamber and the main chapel. There are numerous mosaics on the basilica floor. In the 19th century, the archaeologist Ross detected traces of an ancient harbour at Mastihari.

From Mastihari there are daily connections to Kalymnos by tourist craft.

Opposite page: Kardamaina.
Right and below: the archaeological site at Mastihari and views from the beach.

ROUTE 6
Paradeisos - Ayios Stefanos - Kefalos - Ayios Ioannis

Our sixth and final route around the island begins at Antimacheia and runs along the main road to Ayios Stefanos, Kefalos and the Monastery of St John (Ayios Ioannis).

We leave Antimacheia in a south-westerly direction and enter the **Plaka** area. This is the site of one of the island's most attractive woods. The area has plentiful springs and verdant vegetation and an excursion and picnic site has been laid out.

After passing through the area known as Ammoudies, we continue towards the narrowest part of the island, its 'handle.' Before coming to Kefalos bay, we pass the superb beach of **Paradeisos**, on an attractive stretch of coastline.

Here bubbles of gas rise to the surface of the sea from within the submarine volcanic strata.

We begin by following the coast road to Ayios Stefanos.

Ayios Stefanos is a little village on one of the best beaches which Kos can offer.

It has a particularly interesting double Early Christian basilica of St Stephen (5th century). Each of the two churches (which share a baptistery) has three aisles and is decorated with outstanding mosaics. In front of this double basilica lies the rocky islet known as Kastri, on which there is a tiny monastery to Ayios Antonios.

From Ayios Stefanos, the coastal road leads on to the attractive little harbour of Kamari, with its fishing-boats and caiques. From here, an

Below: the beach at Paradeisos. Opposite page: Views from Kefalos.

unsurfaced track climbs up the mountain to join the main road from Kefalos to the Monastery of Ayios Ioannis.

The stretch of coast between Ayios Stefanos and Kamari is today one of the most important assets of Kos. It is a modern resort area, with hotels, rooms to rent, beaches with amenities, a wide range of sea sports and the Club Med facilities.

The area seems to have been important even early in its history: in antiquity, as can be seen from the archaeological finds, and in the Early Christian period, as we can see from the churches of the area.

The basilicas of Ayios Stefanos, discovered in 1932 by the Italian archaeologist Luciano Lorenzi and dating from 469 and 554, are the most outstanding monuments. They were famed for their wealth, their size and the beauty of their location. The columns were restored by Italian archaeologists after 1932.

From Ayios Stefanos, we climb up to nearby Kefalos, the furthest village from Kos town: 43 km. It has hotels, rooms to rent and restaurants.

The castle above the village was built by the Knights of St John, while the Turks made extensions to it.

Kefalos stands on the most westerly extremity of Kos, on a limestone hill, and its commanding site it topped by a line windmill, known as 'tou Papavasili'. This was once Astypalaea, the island's capital in ancient times. That city was destroyed by earthquake in 413/412 BC, and the remains of a small sanctuary of Asklepios and some of the structures at the harbour are all that have survived. The antiquities found here are kept in the quarter known as Kamari, where parts of the ancient mole can still be seen. The area also preserves

3

remnants of a Hellenistic theatre dating from the 2nd century BC and of temples dating from the same period.

In 1902 archaeological excavations at the location known as Palatia brought to light the foundations of a Doric temple to Demeter. A headless statue of the muse Clio, dating from the Hellenistic period, was also found.

According to the historian Zaraftis, the chapel of Our Lady at Palatia stands in one of the corners of an ancient temple to Dionysus. This church is above the temple of Demeter.

The collection on display in the Kos Archaeological Museum includes a headless statue of the goddess Demeter, seated, and also an enormous head of Heracles, the work of Lysippus, found in the same area.

On the hill known as Ayia Paraskevi above Kefalos are the remains of a basilica. In antiquity, this was the site of an outpost of the deme of Isthmiotes.

Although the Kefalos area does not produce vast quantities of agricultural produce, the qu-ality is high and its honey, pulses, cereals, tomatoes, fruit and vegetables are prized. The inhabitants also have herds of sheep and goats or work as seamen. Barytes and perlite are mined locally.

A road leading out of Kefalos in a south-westerly direction takes us to the furthest extremity of Kos in this direction, where the Monastery of **Aylos Ioannis** stands.

On the way we pass Mt Zini. This is the site of the Aspri Petra cave, where Neolithic finds have come to light. The finds, the oldest ever discovered on Kos, were unearthed and studied by the Italian archaeologist Doro Levi. He came across fossilised human remains, fragments of Neolithic pottery and millstones. The pottery was of a variety of dimensions and a range of scenes were depicted on it. Very few weapons were found. The archaeologists believe that the finds from Aspri Petra date from the Early Bronze Age, although the site was used into the Geometric period as a shrine for rural deities. There is evidence that even in Roman times religious rites were held here.

Our route ends at the Monastery of St John, in an idyllic location, which has its feast day on 29 August (the date when the Decollation of John the Baptist is celebrated).

From Kefalos, a minor road leads north to **Limnionas**, a small natural harbour where there is a well-organised anchorage in which boats can moor during severe storms.

This is the end of our itinerary on the beautiful and interesting island of Hippocrates.

From Kos, we can cross over an become acquainted with the nearby island of Nisyros.

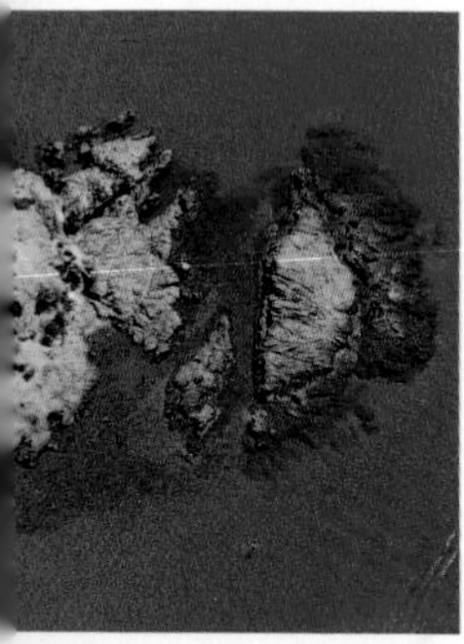

The islet opposite Kefalos and the archaeological site.

NISYROS

Nisyros is one of the smallest of the Dodecanese islands, rich in natural beauties and endowed with an ancient cultural heritage.

The island's monuments, visible with every step, are testimony to its glorious past and affirm the concern of the locals to preserve their cultural heritage and to build a bright and dynamic future upon it.

Nisyros is a place on which natural beauty, the glorious historical past, tradition, popular culture, yesterday and today have come together.

Its majestic volcano, unique among its kind and unrivalled in terms of its natural beauty, immediately impresses the visitor, who gazes at it with wariness and awe.

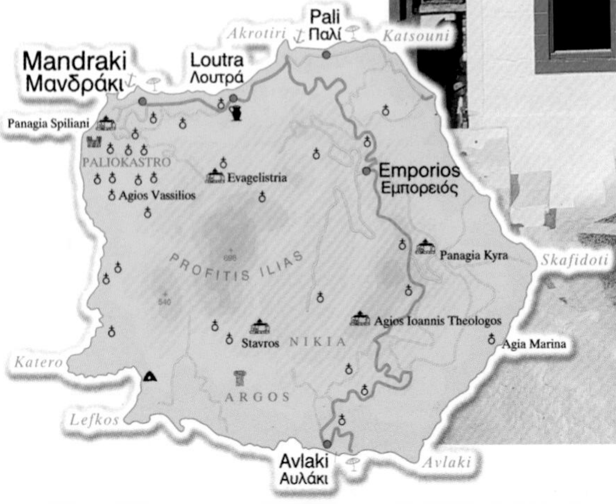

General Information

Nisyros is an island in the south east Aegean, at the centre the Dodecanese group, between the islands of Kos and Tilos and Cape Cnidus in Asia Minor. It lies 8 miles from Kos, 60 miles from Rhodes and 200 miles from Piraeus. The area of Nisyros also includes the islets of Yali (the largest at 5 square kilometres), Ayios Antonios, Strongili, Pacheia, Pergousa and Kandeleousa (Faros).

The area of Nisyros is 41.6 square kilometres. The island is conical in shape and is mostly mountainous, consisting of volcanic rock formations and outcrops of stone produced by the periodic action of the volcano. The volcano formed the Lakkio valley, the craters and the island's mountains: Profitis Ilias 698m, Ayios Ioannis (588 m.) Ayios

Georgios (519 metres).

The geological and tectonic structure of Nisyros has led to the formation of underground springs of hot water which are used for medicinal purposes. The geomorphology of the area and the volcanic nature of the rock formations have also led to the presence of minerals such as perlite, caoline and sulphur compounds and, above all, of pumice stone, which is today the only deposit to be commercially worked.

Among the features of the natural environment of Nisyros are its fauna and flora, which specialists have pronounced to be unique.

In antiquity, Nisyros was famous for its mill-stones; indeed, they were often known as the 'stones of Nisyros.'

The geomorphological feature most characteristic of Nisyros is its volcano, which today is the main reason why most visitors come to the island. The volcano is unique of its kind in Greece, and aside from its scientific interest, is of the greatest beauty. As a result, it is a tourist attraction of the first magnitude. After millions of years of activity, the volcano is now extinct.

Mythology and History

According to the Greek myths, Nisyros was formed as follows. During the Battle of the Gods and Giants, Poseidon, god of the sea, had undertaken the task of eliminating the giant Polybotes; after defeating him, he pursued the beaten giant as he fled in terror across the Aegean in search of a place to hide. Near Kos, Poseidon caught up with Polybotes; with his trident, he broke off a piece of Kos (near cape Chelone or Krikelos) and hurled it at the giant. This flying piece of land pinned Polybotes down; trapped beneath Nisyros as he is, Polybotes sometimes sighs and groans, and this explains the natural phenomenon of the volcano.

Given that Poseidon was responsible for creating Nisyros, it was only natural that he should continue to be its protector. For that reason, there were numerous temples to Poseidon on the island, and its coins often showed the head of the god of the sea.

Another element in the myth is the close bond between Nisyros and Kos - a bond which is still strong even today, and covers the administrative, cultural, social and economic spheres. As we know from numerous inscriptions, there were many Koans on Nisyros, whilst on Kos itself there was a colony of Nisyrians under the name Nisyriadae. The two islands shared a monarch, engaged in military campaigns together, had the same system of government and were members of the same confederations.

The cultural environment of Nisyros, as expressed in the monuments of prehistory and of the Classical, Byzantine and modern periods, is of particular interest for the tourist trade: such cultural elements are natural attractions for visitors.

The earliest monuments on Nisyros date back to the prehistoric period. The acropolis of the ancient city, Palaiokastro, dates from the Classical period and has survived in good condition.

Nisyros also has a wealth of Byzantine monuments, with many Early Christian churches and chapels scattered all over the island. Many have wall-paintings of the greatest interest for historians and visitors. These chapels can be approached along attractive cobbled paths.

Tour of the Island

Visitors who come to Nisyros for the day - which means that they arrive at about 10 a.m. and leave at 4 in the afternoon - will certainly not have the time to enjoy the sights of the island. Their visit will be confined to the volcano and a walk around the village of Mandraki, which certain should not omit the Historical and Folklore Museum of the Monastery of Our Lady Piliani. They will also enjoy swim at the beach called Chochlaki, with its round pebbles.

For visitors who stay on the and, however, the potential is much broader.

One day could be devoted to the volcano, a trip which can be combined with visits to Emborio, Nikia and even Avlaki for those who have transport of their own.

Another day could cover the chapels (such as Our Lady of the Annunciation, the Cross and Our Lady Kyra, in conjunction with lunch and a swim at the attractive village of Pali.

Another interesting set of monuments are the island's Castles of the Knights. The most typical of these is at Mandraki, and it also contains the Monastery of Our Lady Spiliani, founded in around 1600. The main church of the Monastery is dedicated to the Dormition of the Virgin, and the adjacent chapel is to Ayios Halarambos. The icon of Our Lady Spiliani is an outstanding piece of work, and the church also has fine wall-paintings and a rich collective of gold and silver votive offerings. The monastery parlour has a collection of ecclesiastical treasures, and the library contains rare editions.

Emporio is another village with a Castle of the Knights. Inside it is a Byzantine church of the Archangels with important wall-paintings. From the highest point in the village of Nikia there is a superb view of the surrounding islands and down to the volcano.

The Monastery of Our Lady Kyra stands in a position of great beauty and is of archaeological interest. The Monastery has its feast day on 24 August.

The chapel of Our Lady of the Annunciation is only 4 km from Mandraki. A hostel is being constructed there, and it will be possible for nature-lovers who wish to climb Mt Profitis Ilias to stay there overnight. The monastic complex of Stavros ('the Cross') is on a hill to the west of the Lakkio valley, and has its feast day on 14 September. There is another major religious feast at St John the Divine on 26 September.

The most important hot springs are at Loutra near Mandraki, Pali, Avlaki near Nikia and Schiri. Of these springs, those of Pali were known for their medicinal properties as far back as the time of Hippocrates.

One way of touring Nisyros is to take a one-day cruise. The boats land for lunch and a swim at Kormos and Lechies - Pachy Ammos.

Another possibility is a visit to the islet of Yali, where there is a vast beach for swimming and where kakavia, the Greek bouillabaisse, is sold.

In the evening, one can enjoy the seafront tavernas of Nisyros, where the retsina or ouzo ac-company 'pithia' (chickpea rissoles), 'sakkouliasti' (a type of cheese), octopus and whitebait. These tavernas are much frequented by the ordinary people of the island - fishermen, farmers, and quarry workers.

Visitors to Nisyros will have a chance to sample the social and cultural life of the island. They may well be invited to weddings or christenings, or to the feasting which follows. In addition, a large range of folklore and cultural activities take place on Nisyros, especially in the summer months.

Among the local products that visitors can buy as mementoes are 'soumada' (a drink made from almonds) and thyme honey.

Views from Nisyros.

INDEX